D1226488

JUN 2 1 2023

WAR MADE INVISIBLE

ALSO BY NORMAN SOLOMON

Made Love Got War

War Made Easy

Target Iraq (co-author)

The Habits of Highly Deceptive Media

Wizards of Media Oz (co-author)

The Trouble with Dilbert

Through the Media Looking Glass (co-author)

False Hope

Adventures in Medialand (co-author)

The Power of Babble

Unreliable Sources (co-author)

Killing Our Own (co-author)

WAR
MADE
INVISIBLE

How America Hides
the Human Toll of
Its Military Machine

Norman Solomon

THE
NEW
PRESS

NEW YORK LONDON

406 7049

Requests for permission to reproduce selections from this book should
be made through our website: https://thenewpress.com/contact.

Excerpt from "Chant to be Used in Processions Around a Site with
Furnaces" by Thomas Merton, from THE COLLECTED POEMS OF
THOMAS MERTON, copyright ©1963 by The Abbey of Gethsemani,
Inc., 1977 by The Trustees of the Merton Legacy Trust. Reprinted by
permission of New Directions Publishing Corp.

Published in the United States by The New Press, New York, 2023
Distributed by Two Rivers Distribution

ISBN 978-1-62097-791-0 (hc)
ISBN 978-1-62097-805-4 (ebook)
CIP data is available

The New Press publishes books that promote and enrich public discussion and understanding of the issues vital to our democracy and to a
more equitable world. These books are made possible by the enthusiasm of our readers; the support of a committed group of donors, large
and small; the collaboration of our many partners in the independent
media and the not-for-profit sector; booksellers, who often hand-sell
New Press books; librarians; and above all by our authors.

www.thenewpress.com

Composition and book design by Brian Mulligan
This book was set in Sabon MT

Printed in the United States of America

2 4 6 8 10 9 7 5 3 1

The propagandist's purpose is to make one set of people forget that certain other sets of people are human.

—ALDOUS HUXLEY, 1936

The greatest triumphs of propaganda have been accomplished, not by doing something, but by refraining from doing. Great is truth, but still greater, from a practical point of view, is silence about truth.

—ALDOUS HUXLEY, 1946

Do not think yourself better because you burn up friends and enemies with long-range missiles without ever seeing what you have done.

—THOMAS MERTON,
CONCLUDING A POEM IN THE VOICE
OF A NAZI COMMANDANT

CONTENTS

INTRODUCTION

THE DAY AFTER THE U.S. GOVERNMENT BEGAN A ROUTINE of bombing faraway places, the lead editorial in the *New York Times* expressed some gratification. Nearly four weeks had passed since 9/11, the newspaper noted, and finally America had stepped up its "counterattack against terrorism" by launching airstrikes against al Qaeda training camps and Taliban military targets in Afghanistan. "It was a moment we have expected ever since September 11," the editorial said. "The American people, despite their grief and anger, have been patient as they waited for action. Now that it has begun, they will support whatever efforts it takes to carry out this mission properly."[1]

As the United States exploded bombs in Afghanistan during the autumn of 2001, Defense Secretary Donald Rumsfeld's daily briefings catapulted him into a stratosphere of national adulation.[2] The *Washington Post*'s media reporter wrote that "everyone is genuflecting before the Pentagon powerhouse," who was "America's new rock star."[3] During an interview that winter, the host of NBC's *Meet the Press* told Rumsfeld: "Sixty-nine years old, and you're America's stud."[4]

The televised briefings that brought such adulation included masterful claims of notable decency. "The targeting capabilities, and the care that goes into targeting, to see that the precise targets are struck, and that other targets are not struck, is as impressive as anything anyone could see," Rumsfeld asserted. "The care that goes into it, the humanity that goes into it, to see that military targets are destroyed to be sure, but that it's done in a way and in a manner and in a direction and with a weapon that is appropriate to that very particularized target. The weapons that are being used today have a degree of precision that no one ever dreamt of."[5]

Whatever their degree of precision, American weapons were killing a lot of Afghan civilians. Exact numbers were impossible to gauge, but credible estimates hardly called for complacency. The Project on Defense Alternatives concluded that American bombing directly killed more than a thousand civilians during the last three months of 2001.[6] By mid-spring, *The Guardian* reported, "as many as 20,000 Afghans may have lost their lives as an indirect consequence of the U.S. intervention."[7] But regardless of the numbers, the U.S. government was positioned for inherent absolution. Eight weeks after the intensive bombing had begun, Rumsfeld dismissed concerns: "We did not start this war. So understand, responsibility for every single casualty in this war, whether they're innocent Afghans or innocent Americans, rests at the feet of the al Qaeda and the Taliban."[8] In the aftermath of 9/11, the process was fueling a kind of perpetual emotion machine, and there was no off switch.

The Taliban regime fell in November 2001, but the war in the name of stopping terrorism was just getting started. Neither the U.S. mass media nor official Washington had any use for caveats. There was very little interest in what retired U.S. Army general William Odom said on C-SPAN a year later:

"Terrorism is not an enemy. It cannot be defeated. It's a tactic. It's about as sensible to say we declare war on night attacks and expect we're going to win that war. We're not going to win the war on terrorism."[9]

But under the "war on terror" rubric, open-ended warfare was well underway—"as if terror were a state and not a technique," Joan Didion wrote in an essay that appeared as 2003 began, two months before the U.S. invasion of Iraq. Condensing the dominant rhetoric, she described a blot on the horizon: "We had seen, most importantly, the insistent use of September 11 to justify the reconception of America's correct role in the world as one of initiating and waging virtually perpetual war."[10] In one sentence, Didion had captured the essence of a quickly calcified set of assumptions that few mainstream journalists were willing to question.

Those assumptions about the emerging conflicts were catnip for lions of the military-industrial-intelligence complex. Budgets at dozens of "national security" agencies (long-standing and newly created ones) soared along with huge outlays to contractors. They were making fantastic profits, and there was no end in sight as mission creep accelerated into a dash for cash.

The "war on terror" became—for the White House, Pentagon, and Congress—a political license to kill and displace people on a large scale in at least eight countries, rarely seen, much less understood.[11] Whatever the intent, the resulting carnage often included civilians.[12] The dead and maimed had no names or faces that reached those who signed the orders and appropriated the funds. As years went by, it turned out that the point wasn't to win the multicontinent war so much as to keep waging it, a means with no plausible end; the quest, in search of enemies to confront if not defeat, made stopping unthinkable. No wonder Americans couldn't be heard wondering aloud when the "war on terror" would end. It wasn't supposed to.

AFTER 9/11, U.S. MEDIA outlets kept amplifying rationales for an aggressive military response, with the traumatic events of September 11 assumed to be just cause. Voices of shock and anguish, coming from those who had lost loved ones, were emotionally authoritative, and when they endorsed going to war, the message could be moving and motivating. Meanwhile, the president—with almost complete congressional assent—was driving the war train, and religious symbolism was one of the ways to swiftly grease the wheels. On September 14, declaring at the outset that "we come before God to pray for the missing and the dead, and for those who love them," George W. Bush delivered a speech at the Washington National Cathedral. He said that "our responsibility to history is already clear: to answer these attacks and rid the world of evil. War has been waged against us by stealth and deceit and murder. This nation is peaceful, but fierce when stirred to anger. This conflict was begun on the timing and terms of others. It will end in a way, and at an hour, of our choosing."[13]

President Bush cited a story—which he said exemplified "our national character"—being widely told in news reports. "Inside the World Trade Center," Bush recounted, "one man who could have saved himself stayed until the end at the side of his quadriplegic friend." However, a nephew of that man, Abe Zelmanowitz, was unhappy about the context of the president's tribute. "I mourn the death of my uncle, and I want his murderers brought to justice," Matthew Lasar said later that month. "But I am not making this statement to demand bloody vengeance. . . . Afghanistan has more than a million homeless refugees. A U.S. military intervention could result in the starvation of tens of thousands of people. What I see coming are actions and policies that will cost many more innocent lives, and breed more terrorism, not less. I do not feel that my uncle's compassionate, heroic sacrifice will be honored by what the U.S. appears poised to do."[14]

The president's announced objectives were grandiose, with overwhelming affirmations from media, elected officials, and the large bulk of the U.S. public. Typical was this pledge in a speech that Bush gave to a joint session of Congress six days after his sermon at the National Cathedral: "Our war on terror begins with al Qaeda, but it does not end there. It will not end until every terrorist group of global reach has been found, stopped, and defeated."[15]

Yet by late September, as the Pentagon's assault plans became public knowledge, a number of bereaved Americans were speaking out in opposition.[16] Amber Amundson, who lost her spouse, Craig, in the Pentagon, addressed government leaders by writing an article: "If you choose to respond to this incomprehensible brutality by perpetuating violence against other innocent human beings, you may not do so in the name of justice for my husband."[17] Phyllis and Orlando Rodriguez, whose son Greg died in the World Trade Center, said in a public appeal: "We read enough of the news to sense that our government is heading in the direction of violent revenge, with the prospect of sons, daughters, parents, friends in distant lands dying, suffering, and nursing further grievances against us. It is not the way to go. It will not avenge our son's death.

Not in our son's name. Our son died a victim of an inhuman ideology. Our actions should not serve the same purpose. Let us grieve. Let us reflect and pray. Let us think about a rational response that brings real peace and justice to our world."[18] Judy Keane, who lost her husband, Richard, told an interviewer: "Bombing Afghanistan is just going to create more widows, more homeless, fatherless children."[19]

Nor did the president's platform at the majestic cathedral in the nation's capital indicate clear support from prominent clergy. On October 1, a week before the U.S. attack on Afghanistan got underway, Detroit's bishop Thomas Gumbleton noted in a public statement that "the Pope has called for 'peaceful negotiations and dialogue' in the current crisis," and Gumbleton added: "Some have rushed to portray us who are opposed to the Bush administration's plans as naïve and lacking realism. But if you look at the facts, it is clear that it is we who are the realists and those who would rush to war and escalate the cycle of violence are completely out of touch with reality and with lessons of history. . . . The only way to peace is to talk, to negotiate and to build understanding. Yet, President Bush has flatly ruled out the possibility of negotiations and dialogue. What does he hope to gain by issuing ultimatum after ultimatum and refusing to negotiate?"[20]

THE POLITICIZING OF GRIEF exploded in the wake of 9/11. While indescribable pain, rage, and fear set the U.S. cauldron to boil, national leaders promised their alchemy would bring unalloyed security. The gold standard included pursuing a global war effort that promised to be unceasing. America's dead and bereaved were vastly and appropriately important.

In contrast, the deaths and bereavements of equally innocent people, due to U.S. military actions overseas, were devalued to such an extent that domestic politics perpetuated two tiers of grief: momentous and close to meaningless; ours and theirs. The understood boundaries required the leaders of both major political parties to keep affirming and reinforcing the tiers of grief as a kind of zero-sum template. American suffering loomed so large that there wasn't much room to see or care about the suffering of others, even if—or especially if—it was caused by the United States.

Overall, in tandem with Washington's top political leaders, the fourth estate was integral to sustaining the kind of adrenaline flush that made launching a war against terrorism seem like the only decent option, with Afghanistan in the initial gunsights and news outlets filled with calls for retribution. (Officials did not encourage a focus on the U.S. petro-ally Saudi Arabia, the country that fifteen of the 9/11 hijackers hailed from; none of the nineteen hijackers were Afghans.) By the time the United States attacked, twenty-six days after 9/11, the assault could easily appear to be a fitting response to popular demand. Hours after the Pentagon's missiles began to explode in Afghanistan, a Gallup poll found that "90 percent of Americans approve of the United States taking such military action, while just 5 percent are opposed, and another 5 percent are unsure."[21]

With only one in twenty people opposed, such lopsided approval for going to war was a testament to how thoroughly the messaging for a "war on terrorism"—soon often shortened to "war on terror"—had taken hold. It would have been logical, yet nearly heretical, to mention the likelihood that many more innocent people would end up dying as a result of the retribution than had died from the 9/11 mass murder. Routinely, for Americans, the predictable deaths of Afghan civilians would be ignored, downplayed, or discounted as incidental "collateral damage" (a phrase that *Time* magazine had previously defined as "a term meaning dead or wounded civilians who should have picked a safer neighborhood"[22]). The rising civilian death toll was of little or no media consequence.

What had occurred on September 11 remained vividly front and center; what began to happen to Afghan people on October 7 was relegated to, at most, peripheral vision. Amid the righteous grief that had swallowed up the nation in the wake of 9/11, it would be hard to think of words more unwelcome than these from a poem by W.H. Auden: "Those to whom evil is done / Do evil in return."[23]

The events of September 11 on U.S. soil were unprecedented, but what followed had many rough precedents. Direct American military interventions in the previous few decades spanned from Southeast Asia to the Dominican Republic, Grenada, Panama, Iraq, and Yugoslavia—interventions routinely cheered on by journalists and media outlets. Calls to smite the evildoers, by whatever name, were familiar reflexes. Yet the traumas of 9/11 made the United States even more eager and able to present itself as an avenging victim. That stance remained in place as the scope of military operations widened to countries far beyond Afghanistan in the twenty-first century.

Testifying before the Senate Armed Services Committee in September 2002, Defense Secretary Rumsfeld did not miss a beat when Senator Mark Dayton questioned the need for the United States to attack Iraq, asking: "What is compelling us to now make a precipitous decision and take precipitous actions?"

Rumsfeld replied: "What's different? What's different is 3,000 people were killed."[24]

The humanity of people who died on 9/11 loomed so large that the humanity of Iraqi people would be rendered invisible.

AS I SHUTTLED BETWEEN San Francisco and Baghdad, three times in four months before the invasion, I felt that I was traveling less between a pair of countries than between two far-flung planets, connected only via sketchy intragalactic communications. One sphere was increasingly abuzz with debates about when and how to attack, while the other was hoping to survive.

The realistic expectation that many bombs would soon be falling was hard to fathom, looking at ordinary moments of daily life in Baghdad. Eating dinner at an outdoor restaurant along the Tigris River, under the same stars that might be seen from anywhere on Earth, couples and small groups of diners sat at dozens of candlelit tables; the dusk filled with laughter; I stared and thought about how terribly fragile it all was.

The starkest fragility had to do with children. The head of UNICEF's Iraq mission, a Dutchman named Carel de Rooy, proudly described improvements the agency was making at schools in the city. As I could see, the progress was impressive, with the sharp contrast of crumbling schools with glassless windows, buckling floors, and sewage smells, compared to the solid structure and upbeat warmth of a school rebuilt by UNICEF. But the realities of children's health in Iraq remained dire.

After more than a decade of sanctions, UNICEF was in a protracted and desperate battle to save kids' lives. As foreign correspondent Reese Erlich reported when we visited Iraq in the early autumn of 2002, "The U.S.-imposed sanctions have been brutally effective in bleeding Iraqi civilians. For five years, the domestic economy was in a state of near collapse. The medical system was ruined due to lack of equipment and medicines. Public water and sewage systems deteriorated to the point where children regularly suffered gastrointestinal diseases. Malnutrition became a serious national problem. . . . UNICEF estimates that 500,000 children have died as a direct result of sanctions." The rate of malnutrition had dropped during the last few years, but there was far to go; fully one-quarter of the children under five—one million children—were still acutely malnourished. "This is unacceptable," de Rooy said. "More still needs to be done to end the suffering of a generation of children."

But rather than end the suffering of a generation, what was on the near horizon would greatly intensify it. Sitting in his small Baghdad office in December 2002, after de Rooy had described UNICEF's progress in Iraq, I asked what would happen if the expected invasion actually took place. There was a painful silence. Then, quietly, in a few seconds, he said that such a development would be a whole other matter.

Sanctions—inflicted on Iraq by the United Nations at the insistence of the U.S. government—were a form of war by other means, beginning right after the Gulf War quickly took more than one hundred thousand Iraqi lives[25] in early 1991 but left Saddam Hussein's dictatorship in place. With bipartisan support for over a decade, under three U.S. administrations, the sanctions siege had remained largely imperceptible to the American public. A notable and rare jolt to the contrary came one Sunday night in May 1996 during a *60 Minutes* interview with Madeleine Albright, then the U.S. ambassador to the United Nations. CBS correspondent Lesley Stahl brought up the sanctions on Iraq, saying "we have heard that a half a million children have died," and then asked: "Is the price worth it?"

Albright replied, "I think this is a very hard choice, but the price—we think the price is worth it."[26]

The ambassador's maladroit answer caused a bit of a stir. But overall, in U.S. media and politics, dead Iraqi kids remained abstractions. The clumsiness of Albright's momentary candor did not get in the way of her further climb up the diplomatic ladder. Eight months later, she appeared before the Senate Foreign Relations Committee en route to becoming secretary of state. The hearing went smoothly, with some telling moments about U.S. government outlooks on matters of war and peace. "We are not a charity or a fire department," Albright said. "We will defend firmly our own vital interests." But the consummate diplomat was also adept at combining resolute themes with humanitarian notes. Minutes later, she waxed eloquent with these words: "It is said that foreign policy should not be influenced by emotion. That is true. But let us remember that murdered children are not emotions; they are human beings whose potential contributions are forever lost."[27]

The Senate proceeded to confirm Madeleine Albright as secretary of state. If any of the senators were seriously bothered by her statement that causing the deaths of half a million children was "worth it," the lawmakers kept it to themselves. The confirmation vote was ninety-nine to zero.

During many months leading up to the March 2003 invasion of Iraq, news media were routinely closing ranks with Pentagon sensibilities. It was all too easy to replicate the worldviews and jaunty tone of military planners. And so, one evening in November 2002, NPR's already-longtime Pentagon correspondent Tom Gjelten told *All Things Considered* listeners that "a war against Iraq would begin with a bombing campaign, and the resources for that phase of action are largely in place already." He reported: "Defense officials are confident the UN timeline will not get in their way. For one thing, they're going ahead in the meantime with war preparations. Says one senior military officer, 'When the order does come, we have to be ready to rock 'n' roll.'"[28]

BY THE CLOSE OF the century's first decade, for most U.S. media consumers, the overseas wars were becoming rather humdrum news, interspersed with occasional dramatic events. In late March 2010, less than four months after accepting the Nobel Peace Prize, President Barack Obama visited a U.S. air base in Afghanistan[29] and addressed troops while wearing a bomber jacket adorned with an American eagle and the words "Air Force One."[30] At what the *New York Times* the next morning called "a boisterous pep rally,"[31] Obama told the troops as their applause merged with his words: "There's going to be setbacks. We face a determined enemy. But we also know this: The United States of America does not quit once it starts on something. You don't quit, the American armed services does not quit, we keep at it, we persevere, and together with our partners we will prevail. I am absolutely confident of that."[32]

For his latest PR move in a confidence game, it was fitting that Obama spoke at an air base. The long-term trajectory of U.S. war making would involve more reliance on the latest technology in the air and less boots on the ground. The fewer the American soldiers in harm's way, the more abstract the warfare became for the U.S. mass media and its customers—while the appropriators kept voting to fund the wars that fewer and fewer constituents seemed to know about or care much about. The USA's bombing efforts, routinely unreported, extended way beyond Iraq and Afghanistan to also include Pakistan, Libya, Somalia, Yemen, Syria, and elsewhere—in fact, twenty-two countries on four continents.[33] But as far as the American public was concerned, the killing with tax dollars was occurring almost completely out of sight and mind.

"What I'm finding is that the human costs of war have shifted," investigative journalist Azmat Khan, a *New York Times Magazine* contributing writer, told a university symposium in the spring of 2021.

U.S. soldiers, service members, are dying at some of the lowest rates that they have traditionally in history. And the human costs of war are primarily being shifted to both foreign civilians and partner forces. And so this shift to airpower has really taken away some of the political costs that in the past, for example, during the era of Vietnam, have served to curtail war or to mount pressure to end it. So we're really looking at an era of warfare in which the political costs are diminished significantly and those result in far less attention and focus than there would be on wars as in years past.[34]

✧

ON AUGUST 31, 2021, a speech that the White House titled "Remarks by President Biden on the End of the War in Afghanistan" told of plans for greater reliance on airpower as a prudent shift in strategy. "We will maintain the fight against terrorism in Afghanistan and other countries," Biden said. "We just don't need to fight a ground war to do it. We have what's called over-the-horizon capabilities, which means we can strike terrorists and targets without American boots on the ground—or very few, if needed."[35]

The decision to withdraw U.S. troops from Afghanistan brought warfare more into line with the latest contours of domestic politics. The allure of remote-control devices and killing while literally above it all was more irresistible than ever. The political pitch was explicit: "the fight against terrorism" would continue "without American boots on the ground." More than ever, the Pentagon would be tasked with limiting the grief to faraway people who are not us.

Assessing the first twenty years of the "war on terror"— counting only the people "killed directly in the violence of the U.S. post-9/11 wars in Afghanistan, Pakistan, Iraq, Syria, Yemen, and elsewhere"—researchers with the Costs of War project at Brown University estimated those deaths at between 897,000 and 929,000.[36] The numbers, of course, could never begin to convey what the deaths meant to loved ones.

"When scientific power outruns moral power," Martin Luther King Jr. wrote, "we end up with guided missiles and misguided men."[37] Several decades later, Martin Luther King III spoke at a commemoration of his father's birth and said, "When will the war end? We all have to be concerned about

terrorism, but you will never end terrorism by terrorizing others."[38] That was in 2004.

PATTERNS OF CONVENIENT SILENCE and deceptive messaging
are as necessary for perpetual war as the Pentagon's bombs
and missiles—patterns so familiar that they're apt to seem
normal, even natural. But the uninformed consent of the governed is a perverse and hollow kind of consent. While short
on genuine democracy, the process is long on fueling a constant state of war. To activate a more democratic process will
require lifting the fog that obscures the actual dynamics of
militarism far away and close to home. To lift that fog, we
need to recognize evasions and decode messages that are routine every day in the United States.

The nation's faraway warfare draws strength from a dif-
fuse siege on the home front—via media, politics, culture, and
social institutions—more like water on a stone or fumes in the
air than any sudden assault. Living with adherence to don't-
go-there zones, we've become accustomed to not hearing or
seeing what's scarcely said or shown in public. We've grown
acclimated to the implicit assumptions wrapped in daily news,
punditry, and pronouncements from government officials.
What happens at the other end of American weaponry has
remained almost entirely a mystery, with only occasional brief
glimpses before the curtain falls back into its usual place.
Meanwhile, the results at home fester in shadows. Overall,
America has been conditioned to accept ongoing wars without ever really knowing what they're doing to people we'll
never see.

CHAPTER ONE

REPETITION AND OMISSION

THE ESSENCE OF PROPAGANDA IS REPETITION. THE frequencies of certain assumptions blend into a kind of white noise, with little chance for contrary sounds to be heard or considered. In the United States, the dominant media discourse and standard political rhetoric about the country's military role in the world are like that.

Consider the phrase "defense spending." We've heard it countless times. It seems natural. And yes, there is an agency called the Department of Defense (until 1947, the War Department). But an agency's official name doesn't make it true. The ubiquitous use of phrases like "defense budget" and "defense spending"—virtually always written with a lowercase "d"— equates U.S. military operations with defense. But there's a very different side of the story.

How many times have you heard someone on television, or read an article in a big media outlet, saying anything like "Wait a minute. Why are we referring to the Pentagon budget as 'defense' spending? In the real world, the United States spends more money on its military than the next ten countries all together.[1] And most of those countries are military allies."[2] Or, how often have you heard a network anchor mention that the U.S. government currently has 750 military bases operating in foreign countries and territories,[3] compared to no more than three dozen for Russia and five for China?[4] The author of the landmark book *Base Nation*, American University professor David Vine, co-wrote a 2021 report pointing out that "the United States has at least three times as many overseas bases as all other countries combined."[5] The repetition of phrases like "defense spending" is matched by the omission of such inconvenient facts.

When a limited range of information and worldviews is repeated endlessly, that's what dominates the media echo chambers. Meanwhile, the power of omissions—what's hardly ever mentioned—is huge. Protracted silences can be extremely influential.

Key themes, rarely challenged, have continually touted U.S. military might as indispensable for the world. Early in his presidency, Joe Biden was ringing a familiar bell when he declared that America was "ready to lead the world" and "sit at the head of the table."[6]

The militarism that propels nonstop U.S. warfare is systemic, but the topic of systemic militarism gets little public attention. Ballooning Pentagon budgets are sacrosanct. While there can be heated disagreement about how, where, and when the United States should engage in war, the prerogative of military intervention is scarcely questioned in the mass media.

Even when conventional wisdom ends up concluding that a war was unwise, the consequences for journalists who promoted it are essentially nil. Reporters and pundits who enthusiastically supported the Iraq invasion were not impeded in their careers as a result. Many advanced professionally. In medialand, being pro-war means never having to say you're sorry. Journalists who have gone with the war program are ill positioned to throw stones from their glass houses later on; the same holds true for media outlets.

Strong challenges to the status quo of U.S. militarism rarely get into mainstream media. News outlets might provide a significant array of views on many subjects, but there are special constraints on coverage of the Pentagon and its warfare. Exceptions can certainly be found in reporting and commentary on foreign policy and war. But what's exceptional and rare has little impact compared to what's ordinary and routine. Outliers can't compete with drumbeats.

The interwoven media and political establishments stay within what are mutually seen as the bounds of serious discussion. That is especially true of basic war choices. Members of Congress and top officials in the executive branch are acutely sensitive to the reporting and commentary in major media, which in turn are guided by the range of debate at both ends of Pennsylvania Avenue. The right of the United States to militarily intervene in various countries is rarely questioned. Nor do the dominant political and media elites express much concern about the consequences for people living in countries where the United States is making war.

OMISSIONS—WHAT WE DON'T see and hear—might be the most pernicious messages of all.

When routinely included in media, some types of images and themes are magnetic, drawing our attention and whatever thoughts go with it. At the opposite pole, what's omitted pushes thoughts away, providing tacit cues as to what isn't worth knowing or seriously considering.

In media frames, the routine exclusion of people harmed by U.S. warfare conveys that they don't really matter much. Because we rarely see images of their suffering or hear their voices or encounter empathetic words about them, the implicit messaging comes through loud and clear. The silence ends up speaking at high volume: Those people hardly exist. They are others. They are not our concern. They don't particularly matter, while our country is causing their misery.

Opponents of war often contend that antiwar sentiment would grow if news media were to clearly show war's devastating effects. To the shame of major U.S. media outlets, such coverage has been sparse to the point of standard journalistic malpractice in relation to American warfare. The impeding factors include self-censorship, desires for career advancement, and concerns about job security, amid pressures from nationalism, commercialism, and professional conformity.

Contrary to myth, televised coverage of bloodshed in Vietnam wasn't a pivotal factor in turning the public against the war. Actually, very little footage of the suffering and death got on the air. After the last U.S. troops left Vietnam in 1973, *TV Guide* published a series of articles by investigative journalist Edward Jay Epstein, who did an in-depth analysis of all the news coverage by ABC, CBS, and NBC during eleven years of war. In the first half of that period, he found, "producers of the NBC and ABC Evening News programs said that they ordered editors to delete excessively grisly or detailed shots because they were not appropriate for a news program shown at dinnertime."[7] The president of CBS News, Fred Friendly, said that the networks' policies "helped shield the audience from the true horror of the war."[8] As it continued, what did get onto American TV screens hardly swayed the nation.

When communications professor Daniel Hallin methodically went through kinescopes of the three networks' coverage, he found the rough equivalent of Rorschach inkblots: "Vietnam news was ambiguous and contradictory enough, especially after the beginning of 1968, that both hawks and doves could easily have found material to support their own views of the war."[9]

Yet news reporting certainly guides public outlooks. And it mixes with realms of punditry, politics, culture, and entertainment to sustain the continuity of a warfare state. The huge gaps between what actually happens to people in war zones and what we get from the mainline American media are long-standing. Those gaps numb the public and usually protect the political establishment from facing an antiwar upsurge at home. Well-intentioned journalists are confined in a career milieu that filters out the essence of war.

Even when the carnage was at its height in Vietnam, war correspondent Michael Herr later wrote in his book *Dispatches*, the U.S. media "never found a way to report meaningfully about death, which of course was really what it was all about. The most repulsive, transparent gropes for sanctity in the midst of the killing received serious treatment in the papers and on the air." He added that "the jargon of Progress got blown into your head like bullets"—and after wading through the deluge of war-related news stories, "the suffering was somehow unimpressive."[10]

Dynamics varied with later U.S. military interventions, from the quick lightning strikes into Grenada and Panama in the 1980s to the long wars in Afghanistan and Iraq. American media coverage was not monolithic, and as the internet emerged it provided other pathways for information. The secret "Collateral Murder" video from Iraq, officially filmed one day in July 2007 and made public by WikiLeaks in 2010, got to millions of people online.[11] Yet mainstream news outlets still dominated the content and tenor of war coverage reaching the vast bulk of the U.S. population. On the whole, media coverage did little to convey, visually or descriptively, much less viscerally, what war "was all about."

No wonder, as the wars in Iraq and Afghanistan kept going, peace activists yearned for realistic images in news outlets to help turn the militaristic tide. But the barriers in place have included the big flaws in illusions that a media technology could, as the cliché goes, bring war into your living room. The inherent limits of an inanimate device conveying the terrifying chaos of warfare are enough to refute the idea. "What do we see," media analyst Mark Crispin Miller asked in 1988, "when we sit at home and watch a war? Do we experience an actual event?"

In fact, that "experience" is fundamentally absurd. Most obviously, there is the incongruity of scale, the radical disjunction of locations. While a war is among the biggest things that can ever happen to a nation or people, devastating families, blasting away the roofs and walls, we see it compressed and miniaturized on a sturdy little piece of furniture, which stands and shines at the very center of our household. And TV contains warfare in subtler ways. While it may confront us with the facts of death, bereavement, mutilation, it immediately cancels out the memory of that suffering, replacing its own pictures of despair with a commercial—upbeat and inexhaustibly bright.[12]

Even when glimpses and voices of war horrors break through to cause some emotional comprehension among viewers, readers, and listeners, the context of that breakthrough can point conclusions in any number of directions. The moral of the news story and the imagery does not occur in a vacuum. The meaning of the suffering and the belief in the best response to it will be bounded by perceived context; when a photo shows a relative weeping over a bloodied corpse, or when video shows a serviceman carrying a wounded comrade toward a helicopter, the picture might be powerful—but the conceptual frame around it will largely determine the most powerful received message. If the viewer believes that the U.S. war effort is a just and heroic cause, seeing such images of anguish and sacrifice might reinforce a belief in the need to win the war and support America's brave warriors in the process.

"There are many uses of the innumerable opportunities a modern life supplies for regarding—at a distance, through the medium of photography—other people's pain," Susan Sontag observed. "Photographs of an atrocity may give rise to opposing responses. A call for peace. A cry for revenge. Or simply the bemused awareness, continually restocked by photographic information, that terrible things happen." Writing in the fraught era after the October 2001 invasion of Afghanistan and before the March 2003 invasion of Iraq, Sontag noted trending outlooks: "In the current political mood, the friendliest to the military in decades, the pictures of wretched hollow-eyed GIs that once seemed subversive of militarism and imperialism may seem inspirational. Their revised subject: ordinary American young men doing their unpleasant, ennobling duty."[13]

✧

EGGED ON BY RHETORIC from political leaders in Washington, news outlets stoke hero worship of U.S. soldiers engaged in warfare. Glorifying them for serving their country is accepted as a media duty. The U.S. troops and their commanding officers loom large, while the people they kill and wound have no stature. This pseudo-journalistic fidelity to the nation's armed forces and their missions, usually implicit, rises to the unabashed surface at times of military mobilization.

During the 1991 Gulf War, the accolades were unequivocal from the outset. Avuncular CBS journalist Charles Osgood called the bombing of Iraq "a marvel"; his network colleague Jim Stewart helped set the tone by extolling "two days of almost picture-perfect assaults."[14] The network's anchor Dan Rather saw no need to hide his enthusiasm from viewers as he shook hands with the First Marine Division's commander and said, "Again, General, congratulations on a job wonderfully done!"[15] Rather was simply harmonizing with the media chorus while voicing avid support for the massive bombing that was central to the Gulf War, dubbed "Desert Storm" by the Pentagon, a brand—almost hinting at an act of God—frequently and cheerfully parroted by U.S. news media, as though the Pentagon had harnessed a force of nature.

And so, trademarked Desert Storm, the carnage was mass entertainment back home, with unpleasant aspects tastefully omitted. As Sontag wrote, the U.S. military promoted

> images of the techno war: the sky above the dying, filled with light-traces of missiles and shells—images that illustrated America's absolute military superiority over its

enemy. American television viewers weren't allowed to see footage acquired by NBC (which the network then declined to run) of what that superiority could wreak: the fate of thousands of Iraqi conscripts who, having fled Kuwait City at the end of the war, on February 27, were carpet bombed with explosives, napalm, radioactive DU (depleted uranium) rounds, and cluster bombs as they headed north, in convoys and on foot, on the road to Basra, Iraq—a slaughter notoriously described by one American officer as a "turkey shoot."[16]

The media embrace of the upbeat branding and wild fervor for the Gulf War was hardly reduced by grisly photos that showed the remains of Iraqi children who died when an errant American missile struck a Baghdad shelter and killed 408 civilians. Most of the people who died from the attack were burned alive.[17] Days later, NBC's *Today Show* co-host Katie Couric informed viewers that Operation Desert Storm "was virtually flawless."[18] Meanwhile, critics of the war were persona non grata in televisionland. A study by Fairness and Accuracy In Reporting found that during the war only one of 878 on-air sources who appeared on ABC, CBS, and NBC nightly newscasts represented a national peace organization.[19] On the TV networks, with rare exceptions, war victims were not to be seen and war opponents were not heard.

I'VE THOUGHT MANY TIMES about a moment in mid-December 2002 when I was visiting a water treatment plant badly damaged by U.S. bombing of Baghdad during the Gulf War a dozen years earlier. Ever since then, strict sanctions had prevented Iraq from importing vital pumps for such plants on the banks of the Tigris River, and the sanctions also blocked efforts to import chlorine for disinfecting the unsanitary water. The Iraqi guide taking me and a few other foreigners around calmly explained technical matters, until someone asked her about the impending likelihood of a U.S. invasion. Our guide's voice began to tremble. In response, a young American visitor tried to offer comfort, saying: "You're strong."

"No," she responded emphatically. "Not strong." Tears were in her eyes. Moments later she added, "We are tired."

What the Pentagon and U.S. news media were glad to call "shock and awe" came three months later. The spectacular bombing of Baghdad resulted in effusive coverage. One TV network reporter exclaimed to viewers: "Last night a tremendous light show here, just a tremendous light show."[20] With unintended irony, NBC's Tom Brokaw called it a *breathtaking* display of firepower."[21]

The Pentagon announced that it had hospitably "embedded" 750 journalists, who produced media messaging that continually prompted the American public to identify with the bombers rather than with the people who were being bombed.[22] In perceptual effect, the journalists became part of the invading apparatus. And it was through the eyes of the invaders that so much of the reporting was done. As Fox News star Shepard Smith said with perhaps a slip of the tongue, "We have a number of correspondents in bed with our troops across the region."[23] On ABC, anchor Peter Jennings explained that a colleague was "very deeply embedded in a personal way with the Marines he is traveling with." Fox reporter Rick Leventhal later recalled, "We had guys around us with guns and they were intent on keeping us alive because, they said, 'You guys are making us stars back home and we need to protect you.'"[24] Of course, neither Iraqi soldiers nor civilians were being made stars on U.S. networks.

As bombs and missiles continued to explode, few mainline journalists or pundits expressed misgivings. Affirmative news coverage was standard operating procedure. The prevalent outlook accepted without question the absolute right of the United States to bomb Baghdad, a city of five million people, the same approximate human scale as the metropolitan area of Atlanta, Philadelphia, or Houston.

A venerable dynamic was at work, evoking national pride among the superpower's citizens. The quest to justify military action—as some kind of retaliation or preemptive measure—could be implemented in the most emphatic way possible: with the destructive use of overpowering military force.

Four decades earlier, Wayne Morse, a former professor of international law, was one of only two senators to vote against the Gulf of Tonkin Resolution, which opened the bloody floodgates to the Vietnam War in August 1964. That same year, Morse used his raspy voice[25] to insistently declare: "I don't know why we think, just because we're mighty, that we have the right to try to substitute might for right. And that's the American policy in Southeast Asia—just as unsound when we do it as when Russia does it."[26] Yet the temptation to equate military and moral triumphs can be irresistible, as if defeated nations—and the people living there—tell no tales that really matter.

The presumption of high moral ground can require not seeing—or at least not admitting—the base results of actions perpetrated from on high. Reliance on impunity is in sync with preferences for the invisibility of human consequences. If, as a leader, I assume the right to terrorize and kill some people, I might prefer not to see the grisly results—and I would not want the public to see them—especially if those results are not in keeping with my self-image or the image that I want to project for myself and my nation.

TO VICTORS GO SPOILS, only they must not be called spoils. Top U.S. officials categorically rejected assertions that war in Iraq would have anything to do with that country's vast oil reserves. In Washington, government spokespeople were eager to frame oil as a means of establishing Iraqi self-reliance along with limiting Uncle Sam's out-of-pocket expenses. "Iraq is a very wealthy country," said the chair of the Pentagon's Defense Policy Board, Richard Perle, eight months before the invasion. "Enormous oil reserves. They can finance, largely finance the reconstruction of their own country."[27] In the fall of 2003, six months after the invasion, Secretary of State Colin Powell spoke of the need for an equitable return on beneficent services rendered, saying, "Since the United States and its coalition partners have invested a great deal of political capital, as well as financial resources, as well as the lives of our young men and women—and we have a large force there now—we can't be expected to suddenly just step aside."[28]

But some officials became more forthright. Here's a sampling of belatedly candid statements, all from 2007:

"Of course it's about oil, we can't really deny that."[29]
—General John Abizaid, former head of U.S.
Central Command and Military Operations in Iraq

"I am saddened that it is politically inconvenient to acknowledge what everyone knows: the Iraq war is largely about oil."[30]

—Former Federal Reserve chairman
Alan Greenspan, writing in his memoir

"People say we're not fighting for oil. Of course we are."[31]

—Then senator and future Defense
secretary Chuck Hagel

On the tenth anniversary of the invasion, oil expert Antonia Juhasz concluded: "Yes, the Iraq War was a war for oil, and it was a war with winners: Big Oil. . . . Before the 2003 invasion, Iraq's domestic oil industry was fully nationalized and closed to Western oil companies. A decade of war later, it is largely privatized and utterly dominated by foreign firms. From ExxonMobil and Chevron to BP and Shell, the West's largest oil companies have set up shop in Iraq. So have a slew of American oil service companies, including Halliburton,[32] the Texas-based firm Dick Cheney ran before becoming George W. Bush's running mate in 2000."

Juhasz added that "oil was not the only goal of the Iraq War, but it was certainly the central one."[33]

However, candor about oil as a key goal of the Iraq War could only get in the way of PR window dressing for the war effort. To keep the whole house of dissembling cards from falling apart, the touchstone of messaging remained the need to root out terrorism.

America's public discourse is absolutely clear, with moral condemnation of terrorists using crude explosive devices.

The practices of strapping on a suicide belt or loading a car with explosives and then blowing people up are presumed to be the diametric opposite of killing people from the air with the Pentagon's sophisticated technology; one action is beyond reprehensible, another is patriotic service. Potential cognitive dissonance is headed off at the pass with the exculpatory assumption that the situations are entirely different—after all, the terrorist tries to kill innocent people while the U.S. military tries not to. In American media and politics, the distinction is self-evident and axiomatic. But from the vantage point of civilians on the receiving end of the Pentagon's destructive capacities, such distinctions are apt to make no difference.

Authorities want us to believe that the Defense Department carefully spares civilian lives. Yet, during this century, the Pentagon has killed far more civilians than al Qaeda and other terrorist groups have.[34] Without in the slightest absolving those terrorists for their crimes, that reality should give us cause to ponder and reevaluate the standard Manichean autopilot of American thought. A parallel reality also debunks many pretensions about the effectiveness of the "war on terror." During its first twenty years, journalist Nick Turse noted in 2022, "the number of terrorist groups threatening Americans and American interests has, according to the U.S. State Department, more than doubled."[35]

Supporters of the invasion of Iraq tried to justify it as integral to the U.S. fight against terrorism, although Saddam Hussein had nothing to do with 9/11 or al Qaeda. (The invasion actually created the conditions that fostered the formation of terroristic groups such as ISIS.) Regardless, as the occupation dragged on with unanticipated numbers of U.S. troops among the dead and wounded, more commentators back home began to say that the invasion had been an enormous foreign policy mistake. The word "blunder" was often used, as though the main importance of the mass slaughter and devastation was a bad move on a geopolitical chessboard. It was mainly about us. When losses were emphasized, they were singularly American: lives, billions of dollars, and strategic leverage in the region.

DURING FIFTY YEARS AFTER the Vietnam War, the United States grew accustomed to asserting the right and power to make war in a variety of distant countries. Major interventions of the 1980s were confined to the Western Hemisphere— the tiny island of Grenada and then Panama—but those two invasions turned out to be opening acts in a rejuvenating quest for geopolitical dominance. "By God, we've kicked the Vietnam syndrome once and for all," President George H.W. Bush gloated at the end of the Gulf War in 1991, as if public aversion to war making had been a shameful impediment to American glory.[36] Eight years later, President Bill Clinton lauded the USA's leadership in the NATO air war on Yugoslavia.[37] By the turn of the century, political elites and mass media had celebrated an unbroken string of U.S. military triumphs for two decades.

Those decades before 9/11 prefigured the "war on terror." Afterward, the customary wartime features of media boosterism and political bombast went from intermittent to chronic. While the United States was obviously at war in Afghanistan and then Iraq, Libya, and Syria, warfare elsewhere was apt to be a complete mystery for most citizens, even while Pentagon budgets kept climbing. What all that warfare was really doing to Americans got scant attention from media or entrenched politicians, while the actual impacts on people living in the battleground countries were scarcely blips on news screens. Media echo chambers assumed the good intentions if not always the competence of U.S. leaders in the ongoing war that had been vowed against far-flung terrorism. As years went by, a new normal of war footing took hold and tightened its grip on the United States, without any foreseeable end point or need for fresh justification.

CHAPTER TWO

OVER
THE HORIZON

ON THE FIRST DAY OF MARCH 2022, VISITORS TO THE *New York Times* home page saw a headline across the top of their screens in huge capital letters:

ROCKET BARRAGE KILLS CIVILIANS

It was the kind of breaking-news banner headline that could have referred to countless U.S. missile attacks and other military assaults during the previous two decades, telling of civilian deaths in Afghanistan, Pakistan, Iraq, Syria, and elsewhere. But those "war on terror" killings did not qualify for huge banner headlines. What stirred the *Times* to quickly publish one about civilian deaths was—as reported on the front page of its print edition—"a deadly Russian rocket assault on Kharkiv, Ukraine's second-largest city, that raised new alarms about how far the Kremlin was willing to go to subjugate its smaller neighbor."[1]

During the months that followed, the *New York Times* was among thousands of American outlets devoting the kind of news coverage to Russia's war in Ukraine that would have been unthinkable while reporting on U.S. warfare. Early in April, forty days after the Russian invasion began, a jarring headline in all capitals—"HORROR GROWS OVER SLAUGHTER IN UKRAINE"—spanned the top of the front page of the *Times* print edition.[2] During April, fourteen stories on the newspaper's front page "were primarily about civilian deaths as a result of the Russian invasion, all of which appeared at the top of the page," researchers at Fairness and Accuracy In Reporting found. During a comparable period— after the U.S. invaded Iraq—the *Times* published "only one story about civilian deaths at the hands of the U.S. military on the front page."[3]

By any consistent standard, the horrors that the U.S. military had brought to so many civilians since the autumn of 2001 were no less terrible for the victims than what Russia was doing in Ukraine. But the U.S. media coverage was vastly more immediate, graphic, extensive, and outraged about Russia's slaughter than America's slaughter. On the rare occasions when a major U.S. news outlet provided in-depth reporting of civilian deaths caused by American forces, the pieces were usually retrospective, appearing long after the fact—postmortems with little political impact and scant follow-up—hardly making a peep in media echo chambers.

No matter how sophisticated its high-tech weaponry, the large-scale Russian warfare in Ukraine was barbaric. That the same could also be said about American warfare in Afghanistan and Iraq was a truth nearly taboo to utter in U.S. mass media. Both the United States and Russia had brazenly flouted international law, crossing borders and persisting with massive lethal force. Coherent principles would condemn and illuminate each instance. But, despite press freedoms in the United States, very few big-name journalists and their imitators in the profession have been willing to break ranks with the gist of Washington's official war narratives, which are, at bottom, not much more nuanced than assuming that America's exemplary national character has been mobilized to defeat the unmitigated evil of the foe.

Nationalism masquerading as journalism covers war in darkness and light, telling us for whom the bell tolls. And so, when Russia invaded Ukraine and proceeded to terrorize, kill, and maim, the U.S. media were all-hands-on-deck with empathetic, poignant reporting via TV, radio, print, and online outlets. But when American missiles and gravity bombs hit population centers over the previous two decades, the human tragedies rarely got anything more than short shrift in the U.S. media. The extreme differences in the quantity and tone of coverage reflected—and reinforced—the agendas of war makers based in Washington.

In 1996, the National Defense University Press put out a book titled *Shock & Awe: Achieving Rapid Dominance*. The authors—military strategists working under the auspices of a consulting firm led by a former senior Pentagon official—had big ideas for better ways to subdue an enemy nation. "Shutting the country down would entail both the physical destruction of appropriate infrastructure and the shutdown and control of the flow of all vital information and associated commerce so rapidly as to achieve a level of national shock akin to the effect that dropping nuclear weapons on Hiroshima and Nagasaki had on the Japanese," the study said.[4] Its main author, Navy lieutenant commander Harlan Ullman, had taught military strategy at the Naval War College. He was "a scholar in uniform" who was "possessed of one of the best, most provocative minds I have ever encountered," General Colin Powell recalled in his autobiography.[5]

During the run-up to the Iraq invasion in 2003, "shock and awe" became a media meme and a pop-culture fad. "Fascination with Shock and Awe was approaching frenzy," *Air Force Magazine* reported. "No news report was complete without it. Sony applied for a trademark on 'Shock and Awe' to use as the title of a video game but dropped the application in embarrassment when it was discovered by the news media. Others sought to trademark 'Shock and Awe' for pesticides and herbicides, barbecue sauce, and fireworks displays."[6] Stateside, to many, it all sounded groovy and fun. But the American public had been led to expect a quick victory over Iraqi forces, and when that didn't happen the image of "shock and awe" lost some luster.

Nearly twenty years later, when Russia attacked Ukraine, the chief author of *Shock & Awe* quickly assessed what Russia was trying to do to the biggest Ukrainian cities. Ullman judged the Russian effort to be of inferior quality, with mild impact compared to what he had pushed the Pentagon to inflict on Baghdad. "I chaired the group that originated the concept of shock and awe," he crowed in an op-ed piece for UPI a week into the Ukraine invasion. Ullman concluded, "Russian actions are shocking and awing. But they are not shock and awe. Still, who knows how this will end."[7]

Mostly relying on artillery and rockets in tandem with ground troops, Russian commanders were pursuing their mission—widely exposed and suitably denounced in U.S. media. Month after month, Ukrainian people experienced horrible ordeals that were not basically different from what other civilians had experienced in several countries due to bombing by the U.S. Air Force, although any such comparisons were anathema to mainstream media in the United States. For those news outlets, U.S. air warfare was a whole other matter.

AMERICAN MEDIA CONCERN for victims of U.S. bombing has been uncommon. And when top officials bother to address the subject, platitudes combine with stone walls. An unusually blunt twist came shortly after the six-week Gulf War in early 1991, when a reporter asked the chairman of the Joint Chiefs of Staff, Colin Powell, about the death toll among Iraqi people.[8] The question came on the same day that U.S. military sources publicly estimated the figure at one hundred thousand.[9] "It's really not a number I'm terribly interested in," General Powell replied.[10]

Since then, adulation for the Pentagon's airborne arsenal has reached new heights, with media coverage touting the first-rate attributes of the latest weapon systems. Eight months after the March 2003 invasion of Iraq, high up in a prominent front-page article, *New York Times* correspondent Dexter Filkins reported that Black Hawk and Apache helicopter gunships had been flying over Baghdad "with such grace and panache."[11] His near reverence for the latest in U.S. attack helicopters was hardly out of step with other American journalists at major outlets. A central and persistent assumption is that the U.S. government's military capacity should be perceived as an admirable genre of national prerogative—perhaps mistakenly used at times, yet wholly legitimate—the offspring of superior technology married to high moral purpose.

The continual development of high-tech abilities to target and destroy has been supported by large majorities on both sides of the aisle in Congress. As it strikes from the sky, the

United States might seem to be above it all. Occasional bad publicity about an air attack that takes the lives of civilians is typically portrayed as an unfortunate anomaly; if a media uproar ensues, it quickly dissipates.

DISTANT WARS ARE APT to seem only as consequential as their victims. When those who suffer and die are abstractions in U.S. media and politics, so are the wars. And at times, an additional layer of fog sets in when authorities insist that war isn't war at all.

Beginning in the early spring of 2011, the United States led NATO's bombing of Libya, which lasted seven months. The War Powers Act, a U.S. law on the books for several decades at that point, required congressional approval after ninety days.[12] But the Obama administration insisted that the requirement did not apply because the United States wasn't really at war. The White House asserted that what the U.S. government was doing in Libya did not qualify as engaging in military "hostilities" because no Americans were dying in the process.

The first three months of the bombing effort had cost U.S. taxpayers $1 billion, a figure that—along with resulting deaths and injuries—continued to rise during the summer and early fall. Yet the administration kept claiming that it was off the hook with the War Powers Act. After all, American military personnel, in cockpits and behind computer terminals, dropping warheads and aiming missiles at pixels, weren't losing their lives.

The administration's main public voice for that rationale was a former Yale Law School dean, Harold H. Koh, whose current title was State Department legal adviser. His new proximity to government power marked a distance from his prior work far greater than the miles from New Haven to Washington's Foggy Bottom. What startled some observers was not only his novel theory about why a war wasn't a war; Koh had long been a vehement critic of the imperial presidency and a staunch supporter of congressional oversight over war making. His sudden flip-flop stunned many of his former colleagues at Yale. One of them, Professor Bruce Ackerman, noted that "Koh's legal scholarship over the years has been highly critical of presidential overreach on matters of national security, emphasizing the importance of Congress's constitutional powers over war and peace."[13] A professor at Notre Dame's law school, Mary Ellen O'Connell, asked plaintively, "Where is the Harold Koh I worked with to ensure that international law, human rights, and the Constitution were honored during the Bush years?"[14]

In testimony to the Senate Foreign Relations Committee, nine days after the missed deadline for congressional authorization, Koh repeatedly pointed out that the U.S. military was limiting its Libya operations to bombing from the air, as if that fact was exculpatory.[15] It was a mission "involving no U.S. ground presence or, to this point, U.S. casualties," he said. Nor was there "a threat of significant U.S. casualties." (In a fleeting departure from the theme, Koh offered a pro forma throwaway line: "By highlighting this point, we in no way advocate a legal theory that is indifferent to the loss of non-American lives.") Koh's testimony was an effort to square the circle of a self-exonerating legalistic claim: war is not war if Americans kill without being killed. "Whatever his motivations," journalist Paul Starobin wrote at the time, "it is sad to see Mr. Koh, with all his acumen, stretched out on a legal limb so long and so thin that one can almost hear it cracking."[16] But perhaps the most illuminating assessment came from one of the few legal scholars to defend Koh's argument, former Yale colleague Akhil Reed Amar, who said that the United States was not engaged in hostilities in Libya because "there are no body bags" of U.S. soldiers.[17]

WHILE AMERICAN WARFARE IN far corners of the globe remains invisible to the public back home, those operations—backed by U.S. military bases in eighty countries[18]—depend on an Earth-girdling supply chain second to none.

The headquarters for the U.S. Air Force in Europe—the massive Ramstein base in southwest Germany—has functioned as the overseas hub for the airborne power of America's "war on terror," serving crucial functions for drone warfare and much more. "We touch a good chunk of the world right from Ramstein," a public affairs officer, Major Tony Wickman, told me during a tour of the base. "We think of it as a power-projection platform." Soaking up billions of taxpayer dollars, Ramstein has scarcely lacked anything from the home country, other than scrutiny. Its key roles have included relaying video images of drone targets in faraway lands to remote pilots with trigger fingers at computer consoles in Nevada, airlifting special ops units on missions to Africa, and transporting munitions for airstrikes in the Middle East. When I visited Ramstein in 2016, officials proudly told me that the base was meeting transport needs for warfare in Iraq and Syria; during the previous year, those countries were hit by 28,675 American bombs and missiles, according to official data.[19] Back in the United States, voters barely had an inkling as to what such bombing was actually doing to people.

The mystifying fog has been even thicker surrounding Air Force activities south of Europe. The officers I met at Ramstein often mentioned Africa, while the Pentagon remained rigidly unwilling to provide much information about secretive military moves across much of that continent. As early as 2014, the dogged investigative journalist Nick Turse reported that the U.S. military was already averaging "far more than a mission a day on the continent, conducting operations with almost every African military force, in almost every African country."[20] I could see that Ramstein's fleet of newest-model C-130J turboprops was staying busy. With its sleek digital avionics, the cockpit looked impressive. But more notable was the plane's spacious cargo bay, where a pilot explained that it could carry up to 44,000 pounds of supplies or as many as ninety-two Army Airborne "jumpers," each able to be saddled with enough weapons and gear to weigh in at four hundred pounds. From the air, troops or freight—even steamrollers, road graders, and Humvees—could leave the plane's hold under parachutes. Or, according to the Air Force, the agile plane could land on "undeveloped airfields."[21] With Ramstein as its home, the C-130J was proving to be ideal for flying war matériel and special operations forces to remote terrain in northern and western Africa. To what purpose and with what effects? That would be none of your business.

A YEAR AFTER REPORTING on the Ramstein Air Base for *The Nation* magazine, I went in search of military "unmanned aerial vehicles" much closer to home. I found them on a warm spring evening, next to a residential street with trim lawns in upstate New York.

At dusk, I stood and watched planes approach a runway along the other side of a chain-link fence. Just a few dozen yards away, a JetBlue airliner landed. Then a United plane followed. But the next aircraft looked different. It was a bit smaller and had no markings or taillights. A propeller whirled at the back. And instead of the high-pitched screech of a jet, the sound it made was more like . . . a drone.

During the next hour I saw three touch-and-go swoops by drones, their wheels skimming the runway before climbing back above Syracuse's commercial airport. Nearby, pilots were at the controls in front of Air Force computers, learning how to operate the MQ-9 Reaper drone, which had become a key weapon of U.S. warfare from Afghanistan to the Middle East to Africa. Since the previous summer, the Defense Department was using the runway and airspace at the Syracuse Hancock International Airport to train drone operators, who worked at the adjoining Air National Guard base. Officials said it was the first time that the federal government allowed military drones to utilize a commercial airport in the United States. Pilots—steering drones while staring at computer screens—would no longer be confined to remote areas like the Nevada desert.[22]

Activists with the Upstate Drone Action coalition were regularly protesting and being arrested for nonviolent civil disobedience at the adjacent military air base. (Such protests were still happening five years later, in 2022.) But, overall, the takeoffs and landings of "killer drones" at the Syracuse airport got little attention in New York's fifth-largest city. Already routine, the maneuvers were hardly noticed. In an elevator at a hotel near the airport, I mentioned the Reaper drone exercises to an American Airlines flight attendant who had just landed on the same runway as the drones. "I had no idea," she said.

The Reaper drones using the Syracuse runway were unarmed, the Air Force said, but when the trainees went operational they'd be aiming and launching Hellfire missiles at targets many thousands of miles away. To the extent that civic leaders in Syracuse noticed, they embraced the expanding domestic involvement in drone warfare; mention of the human toll far away was a virtual no-no. Elected officials joined with business groups and military public-relations officers in lauding the benefits and virtues. They did not acknowledge that many civilian deaths would result from the extolled activities, or that—in the name of a war on terror—people in foreign lands were being subjected to the terrifying presence of drones overhead. Such matters were a far cry from Syracuse. My random conversations with dozens of the city's residents in many walks of life turned up scant knowledge or concern about the close-by drone operations. In sharp contrast, the metropolitan area's economic distress was front and center.

Unlike the well-financed Air National Guard base, the city's crumbling infrastructure and budgets for relieving urban blight were on short rations. When I talked with people in low-income neighborhoods of Syracuse—one of the poorest cities in the United States—despair was often unmistakable. A recent study by the Century Foundation had identified Syracuse as the city with the nation's highest concentrations of poverty among African Americans and Hispanics.[23] The latest influx of federal largesse was for drone warfare, not for them.

✧

By 2021, the U.S. military had dropped bombs and fired missiles on Iraq for twenty-six of the last thirty years. "It's time we recognize we cannot bomb our way to peace," Win Without War executive director Stephen Miles tweeted.[24] But for U.S. policy makers focusing on nations where American forces were engaged in military actions, peace would be welcome only if other goals could be met.[25]

President Biden chose the week when the last U.S. ground troops were exiting Afghanistan to offer public reassurance that the American military would exercise its "over the horizon" muscle in the future.[26] Whether intentionally targeted or not, the resulting casualties would mostly be indistinct images on aircraft gunsights and computer screens. The president did not mention that remarkable advances in digital technology have enabled the Pentagon to further distance the killers from the killed. He also did not mention that the nation's biggest military contractors were aerospace companies making billions of dollars in profits from the Pentagon's huge shopping list.

During the first two decades of this century, five mega-firms—Lockheed Martin, Boeing, General Dynamics, Raytheon, and Northrop Grumman—divided $2.1 trillion in U.S. military contracts.[27] For fiscal year 2020 alone, the Pentagon provided them with prime contracts totaling upwards of $166 billion. In just that one year, as compensation, the CEOs of those five companies received a total of $105.4 million.[28] The individual and corporate incentives to maintain and gun the war machine are boundless.

The USA's major media outlets very seldom question the

morality of such profiteering; the business model is taken for granted as respectable, even laudable. News accounts are uninclined to detail the massive scale of weapons sales to the Defense Department. Meanwhile, on Capitol Hill, it's rare for lawmakers to decry how much the corporate "defense" sector keeps profiting from war. Under the Biden administration, the trend of escalating military budgets continued, with a large portion of the outlays going to constant innovations in airborne weaponry.

While the two parties fight over major differences on domestic issues, the relations in general have been lethally placid about military spending. When a beyond-bloated Pentagon budget of $768 billion cleared the Senate for fiscal year 2022, the leaders of its Armed Services Committee were both quick to rejoice. "I am pleased that the Senate has voted in an overwhelming, bipartisan fashion to pass this year's defense bill," said the committee's chair, Senator Jack Reed, a Democrat from Rhode Island.[29] The ranking Republican on the panel, Jim Inhofe from Oklahoma, chimed in: "This bill sends a clear message to our allies—that the United States remains a reliable, credible partner—and to our adversaries—that the U.S. military is prepared and fully able to defend our interests around the world."[30]

The bill, which President Biden signed two days after Christmas 2021, also sent a clear message to Pentagon contractors. A few months later, Biden requested a record $813 billion military budget for fiscal year 2023, but that wasn't enough for the Senate Armed Services Committee, which added $45 billion in early summer.[31] Clearly, even greater profits were on the horizon for the nation's military contracting firms.

✧

Early in 2022, four months after President Biden told the UN and the world that the United States had "turned the page" and was no longer at war, the *New York Times* reported that the U.S. military was in the midst of an extended battle with ISIS forces. The first sentence of the story told readers what "the Pentagon said"—that, in the newspaper's words, "American ground forces have joined the fight to retake control of a prison in northeast Syria where Islamic State fighters are holding hundreds of boys hostage."[32] That narrative frame—supplied by U.S. officials and its ally in the conflict, the Syrian Democratic Forces—certainly made the U.S. involvement sound noble, though on closer examination it turned out that an eight-month-old United Nations report had concluded the children at the prison were subjected to conditions of torture and other terrible abuses while under the purported protection of the American ally.[33] But whatever the cruelties inflicted by the Islamic State and the Syrian Democratic Forces, the children were trapped in a horrifying situation as the battle raged around the prison.

The role of the United States was anything but postwar. The *Times* piece, with a Baghdad dateline, reported that "four days of American airstrikes" had already occurred, the fighting was continuing, and the U.S. forces were using "armored Bradley fighting vehicles," while a Pentagon spokesperson in Washington said that "we have provided limited ground support, strategically positioned to assist security in the area." According to the newspaper, "The United States has also carried out airstrikes with Apache helicopter gunships over the past four days to try to break the siege, killing an unknown number of prisoners." The intense battle went on for more than a week. Hundreds of Islamic State fighters were killed, the Just Security project reported later, "even as hundreds more fighters and at least 400 [Islamic State] prisoners are believed to have escaped across the porous border between Syria and Iraq."[34] As the *Times* noted, nearly one thousand U.S. troops remained in Syria "to assist in the fight against ISIS and to protect oil installations."[35] In the spring of 2022, Just Security (based at New York University School of Law) pointed out that "the vast majority of U.S. counter-terrorism operations" going on "across the globe have taken place in secret, outside the realm of public debate."[36] For instance, before four U.S. soldiers were killed by ISIS-aligned forces in the West African country of Niger in October 2021, "most Americans—and even some members of Congress— were unaware that the United States was involved in combat there. A similar lack of public accounting holds true for the U.S. bases in Iraq and Syria that periodically come under attack from Iranian-backed militia groups."[37]

ON FEBRUARY 3, 2022, the *Washington Post* emailed a pre-dawn "Breaking News" bulletin, headlined "U.S. Conducted Counterterrorism Strike in Syria, Pentagon Says; Local First Responders Say Over a Dozen Killed." Below was this summary: "The Pentagon said there were no U.S. casualties for the Wednesday night raid, which it described as successful. The White Helmets group that responded to the scene said it has so far retrieved thirteen bodies, including six children and four women."

By midmorning, the focus of the story had changed dramatically. The *Post* was out with new breaking news. "'This Horrible Terrorist Leader Is No More,' Biden Says After U.S. Raid Kills ISIS Leader," the headline read, followed by an upbeat lead: "President Biden credited U.S. military and intelligence and said they were aided by Syrian Democratic Forces. The raid resulted in the death of Abu Ibrahim al-Hashimi al-Qurayshi—the leader of the Islamic State."

Biden had quickly gone on live television at the White House to claim a triumphant hit. Praising "the bravery of our troops" while emphasizing his role as commander in chief, he said that they were "operating on my orders."[38] While NBC News mentioned that rescue workers had found the bodies of six children and four women—who were "believed to have died in clashes and bombing 'after an American airdrop'"— the network noted that "Biden did not say how many people died in connection with the raid."[39] Throughout the day, administration officials only talked about two children, who they said died after the targeted terrorist set off a bomb that killed his family.

During an extensive interview on *PBS NewsHour* that evening, deputy national security adviser Jonathan Finer led off by taking a victory lap about the killing of the ISIS leader, referring to him by his nom de guerre, Hajji Abdullah. Then anchor Judy Woodruff made Finer's appearance a bit uncomfortable.

WOODRUFF: I want to ask you, Jon Finer, about the death of civilians involved, family members. I know the president said today everything possible was done to avoid that. . . . My question is, was everything possible done to avoid that, or is the decision simply made, since these innocents are so close to the target, this is just part of doing business?

FINER: Well, what I can say, Judy, is that from the very beginning, from the moment the president was first briefed on this operation, frankly from the moment the operation began being planned months ago, the desire to avoid at almost in every way civilian casualties was foremost in the minds of the planners, of the president himself, and I know of the service members who took part in this operation. That is a major part of why this was not a drone strike that took place against this target, we put U.S. service members on the ground in harm's way to conduct this action precisely to avoid civilian casualties. This is why when they arrived at the target, they gave the people inside every opportunity to come out of the house and be detained as opposed to a different outcome. And what Hajji Abdullah, the terrorist who we were just discussing, chose to do instead was to blow up the third floor of the building where he was living with his family, cave in the roof, and cause significant harm and damage to the civilians inside.

WOODRUFF: At the same time, Jon Finer, we know there've been a pattern of airstrikes where civilians have died, there's frankly also been reporting on dissembling by the military about what's happened in these situations. How can the American people have confidence that we're getting the straight story from the military now?

FINER: Well, I think you've seen the leadership of the

Pentagon stand up and talk about the fact that they know that there've been issues in the past and they are taking significant steps to try to get their arms around this issue, and announced some improvements and steps they're taking to make sure that these incidents are minimized to the greatest extent possible going forward as they were in this case. But what I can say is, the accounts that we have of this incident are drawn from eyewitness accounts, from the service members who were on the site, not from people who showed up afterwards and tried to assess what happened based on what they encountered. And I think those reports, from our most experienced, most professional, most capable service members are highly credible.[40]

The *NewsHour* interview with Finer was a bit unusual; U.S. government officials are not often pressed in major media venues to defend the military's killing of civilians. Yet the interview was also fairly typical of what happens on the infrequent occasions when a media spotlight falls on such killings and journalists actually raise some pointed questions. Most officials are well versed in techniques of obfuscation.

The civilian deaths that Finer tried to downplay came six days after Defense Secretary Lloyd Austin ordered an "action plan" while declaring in a memo: "The protection of civilians is fundamentally consistent with the effective, efficient and decisive use of force in pursuit of U.S. national interests, and our efforts to mitigate and respond to civilian harm are a direct reflection of U.S. values. It is a strategic and a moral imperative."[41] Austin was engaged in a timeworn Pentagon PR exercise of pledging to fix what could not really be fixed, given the military's actual priorities. The American Civil Liberties Union responded, "What's needed is a truly systemic overhaul of our country's civilian harm policies to address the massive structural flaws, likely violations of international law, and probable war crimes that have occurred in the last twenty years. Any comprehensive review also needs to address and end unlawful and unaccountable lethal strikes even outside of warzones. Actions will speak louder than words, and we need urgent action to end twenty years of war-based approaches that have caused devastating harm to Muslim, Brown, and Black civilians around the world."[42]

After the new Pentagon vow, an incisive reaction came from journalist Peter Maass, drawing on his experience as a war correspondent. "From the beginning, one of the hallmarks of the post-9/11 wars has been the widely reported killing of civilians by U.S. forces," Maass wrote. As for "the Pentagon's protestations of disappointment at what has happened, and its promises to do better," he added, they were "the standard confetti of insincerity. . . . The important thing to watch is not what powerful institutions promise to do but what they actually do. And when they do nothing after promising again and again to make changes, you would be foolish to regard their latest vow as meaningful."[43]

At the Institute for Policy Studies, author Phyllis Bennis offered this assessment in 2022: "The so-called 'global war on terror' has, from its origins, been characterized by attacks by U.S. Special Forces, by airstrikes, by armed drones, and more, that routinely kill far more civilians than the targets identified on the 'kill lists' prepared by presidents and top White House officials. The routine recitation of 'there is no military solution to terrorism' has always been an anodyne rhetorical ploy, never an actual guide to what actions might actually work to change the conditions that give rise to terrorism."[44]

CHAPTER THREE

UNINTENDED
DEATHS

UNLIKE TERRORIST GROUPS SUCH AS AL QAEDA AND THEIR jihadist leaders, the U.S. government and its war planners do not deliberately kill civilians. But, for those killed and for their loved ones, the contrast can be a distinction without a difference.

While the Pentagon's forces do not kill noncombatants on purpose, such deaths are predictable. One factor: U.S. troops can be hazy or even clueless about whether the people they're killing are civilians. A year after the invasion of Iraq, amid growing resistance to the occupation, *Time* reported: "In some neighborhoods, the Marines say, anyone they spot in the streets is considered a 'bad guy.'" The magazine quoted Major Larry Kaifesh: "It is hard to differentiate between people who are insurgents or civilians. You just have to go with your gut feeling."[1]

Frequent killing of civilians is inherent in the types of wars that the United States has waged in this century. Despite all the hype about precision weaponry, even its top-rated technologies are fallible. What's more, they operate in flawed— and sometimes highly dysfunctional—contexts. Whether launching attacks from distant positions or directly deployed, American forces are far removed from the societies they seek to affect. Key dynamics include scant knowledge of language, ignorance of cultures, and unawareness of such matters as manipulation due to local rivalries.

When U.S. officials say that civilian deaths are merely accidental outcomes of the war effort, they don't mention that such deaths are not only predictable—they're also virtually inevitable as results of policy priorities. Presumptions of acceptability are hot-wired into the war machine. The lives taken, injuries inflicted, traumas caused, environmental devastation wrought, social decimation imposed—all scarcely rank as even secondary importance to the power centers in Washington.

In your local community, imagine how you would feel if police made a practice of spraying gunfire through the front windows of stores and other public locations while chasing criminals. Such efforts would surely take the lives of innocent bystanders—yet none of them would be "targeted." And so their wounds and deaths could always be called unfortunate accidents and mistakes.

A steady flood of lofty rhetoric from the White House and Capitol Hill has emphasized the best of intentions throughout the "war on terror." In contrast to terrorists, we are made to understand, the U.S. government strives to safeguard rather than take the lives of civilians. Unmentioned are estimates like the one from Brown University's meticulous Costs of War program that conservatively put the number of civilians killed "directly in the violence of the U.S. post-9/11 wars" at upwards of 364,000 during the first two decades.[2]

Implausible deniability is routine—for the president, the Pentagon brass, State Department officials, congressional leaders—as they refuse to acknowledge that ongoing civilian deaths are integral to the "war on terror." While American forces are supposed to distinguish between terrorists and the terrorized, such distinctions easily get lost in countries where people of all ages experience the U.S. military itself as terrifying. The Americans can make and break their own rules, operating as intruders who are unaccountable for the results of their violence, no matter how indiscriminately lethal. Yet the Pentagon can always say that maimed and killed civilians were not targeted; in each instance, the shattering of their lives was just a tragic error.

FOR STANDARD MEDIA PUNDITRY, the agonies and fatalities due to U.S. firepower have been irrelevant to the nation's tasks at hand. Even statements verging on advocacy of war crimes are not apt to raise eyebrows. *New York Times* columnist Thomas Friedman started off 1998 with a call for "bombing Iraq, over and over and over again."[3] In early 1999, his list of policy prescriptions included: "Blow up a different power station in Iraq every week, so no one knows when the lights will go off or who's in charge."[4] Such disruptions of electricity would have deadly effects, from Iraqi hospitals to the homes of vulnerable civilians, preventing refrigeration of essentials like medicine and food while endangering water supplies.

As for the air war on Yugoslavia in 1999, Friedman was gung ho as it continued in early April, writing, "Twelve days of surgical bombing was never going to turn Serbia around. Let's see what twelve weeks of less than surgical bombing does. Give war a chance."[5] Another column included a gleeful approach of threatening civilians in Serbia with protracted terror: "Every week you ravage Kosovo is another decade we will set your country back by pulverizing you. You want 1950? We can do 1950. You want 1389? We can do 1389 too."[6] As so often happens, the spin from staff-written news articles and outlooks from staff columnists were quite compatible as the war against Yugoslavia continued. "NATO began its second month of bombing against Yugoslavia today with new strikes against military targets that disrupted civilian electrical and water supplies"—the first words of the lead article on the *New York Times* front page the last Sunday in April 1999—promoted the remarkable concept that the bombing disrupted "civilian" electricity and water yet the targets were "military."[7] Never mind that such destruction of infrastructure would predictably lead to outbreaks of disease and civilian deaths. On the newspaper's opinion page, Friedman made explicit his enthusiasm for destroying civilian necessities: "It should be lights out in Belgrade: Every power grid, water pipe, bridge, road and war-related factory has to be targeted." He pointed to a big silver lining in the war's thunderclouds. "While there are many obvious downsides to war-from-15,000-feet, it does have one great strength—its sustainability. NATO can carry on this sort of air war for a long, long time. The Serbs need to remember that." And so, "if NATO's only strength is that it can bomb forever, then it has to get every ounce out of that. Let's at least have a real air war."[8]

Even more telling than Friedman's avid heartlessness was his undiminished—and actually enhanced—stature among colleagues in the media establishment. That esteem was underscored three years later when Friedman won the Pulitzer Prize for commentary.

✧

WHEN THE UNITED STATES LED NATO's aerial bombing of Serbia and Kosovo in 1999, the seventy-eight straight days of bombardment won wide media acclaim at home, while grisly outcomes received, at most, fleeting ink and airtime. Among the routinely overlooked aspects of the air war was the use of CBU-87/B "combined effects munitions," more commonly known as cluster bombs. Weighing in at one thousand pounds, those warheads were notably horrific, though you'd never have known it from the triumphalist words of NATO's supreme allied commander, General Wesley Clark, and President Bill Clinton. When troubling news slipped through—which rarely happened—media consumers had good reasons to be appalled.

On the first Friday in May, at noontime, NATO forces dropped cluster bombs on the city of Niš, in the vicinity of a vegetable market. "The bombs struck next to the hospital complex and near the market, bringing death and destruction, peppering the streets of Serbia's third-largest city with shrapnel," a dispatch in the *San Francisco Chronicle* reported. "In a street leading from the market, dismembered bodies were strewn among carrots and other vegetables in pools of blood. A dead woman, her body covered with a sheet, was still clutching a shopping bag filled with carrots."[9] Pointing out that cluster bombs "explode in the air and hurl shards of shrapnel over a wide radius," BBC correspondent John Simpson wrote in the *Sunday Telegraph*: "Used against human beings, cluster bombs are some of the most savage weapons of modern warfare."[10] But savagery hardly precluded using them.

Midway through the air war, *Los Angeles Times* journalist Paul Watson reported from Pristina, where hospital doctors said they had already treated several hundred people—about half of them civilians—injured by cluster bombs since the start of the war: "During five weeks of airstrikes, witnesses interviewed here say, NATO warplanes have dropped cluster bombs that scatter smaller munitions over wide areas. In military jargon, the smaller munitions are bomblets. Dr. Rade Grbic, a surgeon and director of the main hospital in Pristina, the capital of Kosovo, sees proof every day that the almost benign term bomblet masks a tragic impact." The dispatch quoted Grbic, who said, "I have been an orthopedist for 15 years now, working in a crisis region where we often have injuries, but neither I nor my colleagues have ever seen such horrific wounds as those caused by cluster bombs. They are wounds that lead to disabilities to a great extent. The limbs are so crushed that the only remaining option is amputation. It's awful, awful." The doctor added: "Even when all of this is over, it will be a big problem because no one knows the exact number of unexploded bombs."[11]

For the vast majority of the U.S. public—encouraged by news media and political leaders to take pride in the extensive bombing of Yugoslavia—such awful human realities were imperceptible.[12] And it was a simple, noncontroversial matter less than three years later when the U.S. military dropped cluster bombs on Afghanistan during the invasion and initial phase of occupying that country. The Pentagon's forces proceeded to fire cluster munitions on a large scale in Iraq, without blowback in the United States. The official Congressional Research Service later noted that "U.S. and British forces used almost thirteen thousand cluster munitions containing an estimated 1.8 million to two million submunitions during the first three weeks of combat in Iraq in 2003."[13]

But when Russia used cluster munitions during its 2022

invasion of Ukraine, it was a whole different story. Suddenly, American media put those horrible weapons in a glaring spotlight. On March 1, the print edition of the *New York Times* front-paged a news account that referred to "internationally banned cluster munitions" in the second paragraph and went on to report, "Neither Russia nor Ukraine is a member of the treaty that bans cluster munitions, which can be a variety of weapons—rockets, bombs, missiles and artillery projectiles—that disperse lethal bomblets in midair over a wide area, hitting military targets and civilians alike."[14] But nowhere did the long article include some basic facts that might have knocked Uncle Sam off a high horse. For one thing, the United States was *also* not "a member of the treaty that bans cluster munitions." For another, the prominent 1,570-word *Times* story failed to mention anything about the U.S. military's repeated use of cluster munitions during its own invasions and other warfare.

Several days later, still without any mention of the U.S. government's refusal to sign the treaty banning cluster munitions, the *Times* published an article under the headline "NATO Accuses Russia of Using Cluster Bombs in Ukraine." The piece buried a single sentence about the United States' record at the very end of a twenty-four-paragraph article on page 9, telling readers: "NATO forces used cluster bombs during the Kosovo war in 1999, and the United States dropped more than 1,000 cluster bombs in Afghanistan from October 2001 to March 2002, according to a Human Rights Watch report."[15]

NBC Nightly News was no better. The program did tell its more than 7 million viewers that cluster munitions are "banned by 110 countries, though not by Russia or the U.S." But network correspondent Matt Bradley quickly—and falsely—added: "Still, the U.S. hasn't used them since the first Gulf War, over thirty years ago." The NBC reporter was off by eighteen years.[16]

While reporting on Russia's use of cluster munitions, very few U.S. news outlets noted that American invading forces had used them in Afghanistan and then in Iraq.[17] And almost never mentioned was the Tomahawk missile attack with a cluster bomb that killed fourteen women and twenty-one children in Yemen a week before Christmas in 2009.[18] The missile was fired from a U.S. Navy warship.[19]

The time did come when top government officials and mass media in the United States finally condemned cluster munitions with widespread moral outrage—when Russia used them in 2022. But for America's political elites and major media outlets, civilians whose bodies had been shredded by U.S. cluster bombs were as forgettable as they'd been invisible.

IN EARLY 2009, the United States entered into what could be called Endless War 2.0, as the new president escalated warfare in Afghanistan and continued the war in Iraq—making the precepts of perpetual war explicitly bipartisan. Meanwhile, out of the political and media spotlights, U.S. bombing and special ops efforts persisted in countries that seldom made it to back pages let alone front pages.

Barack Obama had been president for only ten days when Bill Moyers used his PBS program to point out that the Afghanistan war was on the verge of entering a new and ominous stage. Moyers's long stint as a top aide to President Lyndon Johnson during the escalation of the Vietnam War gave unspoken and added weight to his words. "Very often in the

White House, the most momentous decisions are, at the time, the least dramatic, the least discussed," Moyers said. "And they don't make news, or history, until much later, when their consequences bubble to the surface downstream. There are observers who think that could prove to be the case with a decision made within hours of Barack Obama's swearing in last week." Already, Obama had sent Predator drones into Pakistan, where (the London *Times* reported) "three children lost their lives" and missiles destroyed several homes. In recent months, Moyers said, "thirty-eight suspected U.S. missile strikes have killed at least 132 people in Pakistan, where allegedly we are not at war."[20] Statements from officials in the new administration foreshadowed that such attacks in a number of countries would be routine.

That the routine would include a pattern of killing civilians from the air was far from a secret. Moments after Moyers introduced former Pentagon official Pierre Sprey, identifying him as "one of Defense Secretary Robert McNamara's famous 'whiz kids,'" Sprey was unequivocal about deaths to be imposed on noncombatants. "I have no doubt," he said, that the goal of U.S. officials was "to strike militants." But, Sprey added, "I'd be astonished if one in five people they kill or wound is in fact a militant. You can't tell with a camera or an infrared sensor or something whether somebody's a Taliban. In the end, you're relying on either, you know, some form of intercepted communications, which doesn't point at a person. It just, you know, points at a radio or a cell phone or something like that. Or, most likely, you're relying on some Afghani of unknown veracity and unknown motivation and who may, may very well be trying to settle a blood feud rather than give you good information."

Moyers responded with a question: "But don't these drone planes and Predator missiles provide a commander-in-chief, a president of the United States, with enormous political convenience for being able to order military action without risking American lives?"

"Yes," Sprey replied. He added that "bombing is always politically popular, relative to sending infantry and killing our boys."[21]

FROM THE AIR, looking out on a vast panorama of sandy-colored mountains and valleys near Kabul, I wondered, *Where are the trees?* They were gone—destroyed by war and deprivation—banished by countless bombs and the collapse of irrigation. The streets of Kabul were blowing with harsh dust, a harvest of war. Men brandishing M16s were all over the place.

It was late summer in 2009. Days after landing, I met a girl named Guljumma. She was seven years old, living at a place called Helmand Refugee Camp District 5, on the outskirts of Kabul.

Guljumma talked about what happened one morning the previous year: She was sleeping at home, in southern Afghanistan's Helmand Valley. At about five a.m., bombs exploded. Some people in her family died. She lost an arm.

With a soft, matter-of-fact voice, Guljumma described those events. Her father, Wakil Tawos Khan, sat next to her. He took out copies of official forms that he had sent to the Afghan government. Like the other parents who were gathered inside their crude tent in this squalid camp, Khan hadn't gotten anywhere by going through channels. He was struggling to take care of his daughter. And he had additional duties as a representative for a hundred or so of the families in the camp, which was little more than ditches, mud structures, and ragged canvas.

Guljumma's father pointed to a plastic bag containing a few pounds of rice. It was his responsibility to divide the rice for the families. Basics like food arrived at the camp only sporadically, Khan said. Donations came from Afghan businessmen. The government of Afghanistan was doing very little. The United Nations didn't help. Neither did the U.S. government.

Khan emphasized his eagerness to work. We have the skills, I heard him say via a translator—give us some land and just dig a well, and we'll do the rest. From the sound of his voice, hope was fraying.

I thought, *The last time Guljumma and her father had meaningful contact with the U.S. government was when it bombed them.*

I looked around the refugee camp and thought about how it was apparently out of the question for my government to spend the equivalent of the cost of a single bomb to assist the people desperately living there.

IN WASHINGTON, POLICY MAKERS haven't wanted to talk about human impacts of the military's high-tech wizardry. Yet consider these words from a Pakistani photographer, Noor Behram, describing the aftermath of a U.S. drone attack: "There are just pieces of flesh lying around after a strike. You can't find bodies. So the locals pick up the flesh and curse America. They say that America is killing us inside our own country, inside our own homes, and only because we are Muslims."[22] Also unseen and uncomprehended by Americans is the continual terror their government causes. Consider these words from former *New York Times* reporter David Rohde, recalling his captivity by the Taliban in tribal areas of Pakistan: "The drones were terrifying. From the ground, it is impossible to determine who or what they are tracking as they circle overhead. The buzz of a distant propeller is a constant reminder of imminent death." And: "Drones fire missiles that travel faster than the speed of sound. A drone's victim never hears the missile that kills him."[23]

For the United States, the latest weapon technologies are very valuable for off-loading moral culpability from public agendas; little muss, less fuss.

DURING THE OBAMA PRESIDENCY, Lisa Ling was among several veterans of the U.S. drone program who went public with vehement opposition to it.[24] "I would like to see humanity brought into the political discourse," she told me, moments after we met at a coffee shop not far from the Golden Gate Bridge. Her two decades of work for the military had included a few years acclimating Air National Guard personnel to the Air Force's use of drones. Intense remorse came later. "We are in the United States of America and we are participating in an overseas war, a war overseas, and we have no connection to it other than wires and keyboards," she told a documentary filmmaker. "Now, if that doesn't scare the crap out of you, it does out of me. Because if that's the only connection, why stop?"[25]

During the Biden presidency, former tech sergeant Ling was still speaking to journalists about what it was like to look at blurry images on screens and target people. "The truth is that we could not differentiate between armed fighters and farmers, women, or children," she told a writer for *MIT Technology Review*, who quoted her in a late 2021 article headlined "After 20 Years of Drone Strikes, It's Time to Admit They've Failed."[26] As someone with extensive direct knowledge of lethal drone operations, Ling was extraordinary not because of her conclusions but because of her willingness to keep saying them out loud without anonymity. Glimpses of such realities usually came from unnamed sources. And so, an officer willing to be identified only as "an Air Force colonel with firsthand experience of the drone program" told the Washington editor of *Harper's Magazine*: "If you want to know what the world looks like from a drone feed, walk around for a day with one eye closed and the other looking through a soda straw. It gives you a pretty narrow view of the world."[27]

Whatever its purported efficacy, the moral failure of the Pentagon's drone program has been well established—not only by a profusion of firsthand, eyewitness accounts but also by classified documents. Much information became public knowledge thanks to whistleblower Daniel Hale, who served in the U.S. Air Force from 2009 to 2013, briefly worked for a military contractor afterward, and went on to blow the cover off the government's drone warfare with its own documents—refuting deceptions and dispelling illusions about the drone system.[28] The classified documents from Hale enabled *The Intercept* to publish a series of illuminating articles in October 2015. "The White House and Pentagon boast that the targeted killing program is precise and that civilian deaths are minimal," one of the pieces reported. "However, documents detailing a special operations campaign in northeastern Afghanistan, Operation Haymaker, show that between January 2012 and February 2013, U.S. special operations airstrikes killed more than 200 people. Of those, only thirty-five were the intended targets. During one five-month period of the operation, according to the documents, nearly 90 percent of the people killed in airstrikes were not the intended targets. In Yemen and Somalia, where the U.S. has far more limited intelligence capabilities to confirm the people killed are the intended targets, the equivalent ratios may well be much worse."[29]

Brandon Bryant—a former Air Force sensor operator who participated in drone attacks on Iraq, Afghanistan, Pakistan, Yemen, and Somalia for five years while stationed in New Mexico and Nevada—became an outspoken opponent of drone warfare as early as 2012.[30] Four years later, he told me he'd concluded that the entire system for drone attacks was set up "to take away responsibility, so that no one has responsibility for what happens." Other drone whistleblowers reached similar conclusions while deciding to take back some responsibility. A former Air Force drone technician, Cian Westmoreland, was stationed in Afghanistan at the Kandahar Air Field, where he helped build a signal relay station that connected to the Ramstein base in Germany. He never moved a joystick to maneuver a drone and never pushed a button to fire a missile. Yet, back home as a civilian, Westmoreland spoke sadly of the commendations he received for helping to kill more than two hundred people with drone strikes. "I did my job," he said, "and now I have to live with that."

Near the end of 2013, Heather Linebaugh authored an article for *The Guardian* that recounted her experiences as a drone operator and analyst for the U.S. military. Linebaugh wrote that she and her colleagues "always wonder if we killed the right people, if we endangered the wrong people, if we destroyed an innocent civilian's life all because of a bad image or angle." For politicians defending the drone program, at the time formally known as the "Unmanned Aerial Vehicle Predator and Reaper program," she put forward a few anguished questions, such as "How many women and children have you seen incinerated by a Hellfire missile?" And "How many men have you seen crawl across a field, trying to make it to the nearest compound for help while bleeding out from severed legs?"[31]

My conversations with drone whistleblowers left me thinking about the huge gaps between how war "issues" are commonly discussed in the United States and what they actually mean for actual people. Journalism, or what passes for it, rarely does much to go below surfaces. Abstractions, clichés, evasive silences isolate us from agonizing human experiences.

"We're moving towards more network-centric warfare," Westmoreland told me. "So, orders [are] dealt out over a network, and making systems more autonomous, putting less humans in the chain. And a lot of the positions are going to be maintenance, they're technician jobs, to keep systems up and running." An emerging process desensitizes to the point of grim dehumanization. As Andrew Cockburn wrote in his book *Kill Chain*, "there is a recurrent pattern in which people become transfixed by what is on the screen, seeing what they want to see, especially when the screen—with a resolution equal to the legal definition of blindness for drivers—is representing people and events thousands of miles and several continents away."[32]

When drone specialist Ling says that "we would not differentiate between armed fighters and farmers, women, or children," she is also saying that people who kill are not seeing the people they kill. In ways at once less and more direct, that is also true of the commander in chief and every Congress member who votes for war appropriations. Meanwhile, the systems of remote killing get major help from reporters, producers, and editors who detour around the carnage at the other end of U.S. weaponry.

Whether they are actively engaged or passively disengaged, there are counterpoints between the outlooks of distant drone pilots and of Americans who may glance at their country's warfare through the media sights of news outlets. Drone pilots are often psychologically traumatized; at the same time, news watchers are numbed, with deaths, injuries, traumas, made obscure to the point of unreality. The drone operators see in real time with delays of just a few seconds, while U.S. media customers look into a kind of warp that disassociates from what their government is doing. And truly, the war system doesn't really care what you think about it; the war system only cares what—if anything—you might do about it.

ZAMARAI AHMADI WAS ONE of ten family members—including seven children—killed by a drone strike as a parting shot by the U.S. military while withdrawing from Afghanistan in August 2021.[33] Ten weeks later, Reuters reported, "An investigation by the U.S. military's inspector general said that although the strike was a mistake, it was not a case of criminal negligence and that disciplinary action was not recommended."[34] *USA Today* called it a "tragic error" while summing up the assessment by the Air Force inspector general, Sami Said; in the newspaper's words, Lieutenant General Said concluded that "the strike did not break any laws." He called it "an honest mistake."[35]

More authoritative absolution came in mid-December, when Defense Secretary Lloyd Austin approved a recommendation that no one face any disciplinary action for the killing of the ten civilians.[36] The Pentagon followed up by deploying spokesperson John Kirby to do damage control. Appearing on MSNBC, he said: "We looked at this thing very very comprehensively, and again we acknowledge that there were procedural breakdowns, processes were not executed the way they should have been. But it doesn't necessarily indicate that an individual or individuals have to be held to account for that. . . . There's not going to be individual discipline as a result of this really."[37]

In contrast, punishment was sure to come for drone whistleblower Daniel Hale. In July of 2021, he hand-printed a five-page letter to the judge who would soon sentence him to several years in prison. He had given documents to the press, he wrote, "not one more nor one less than necessary, to dispel the demonstrable lie that said drone warfare kept us safe, that our lives are worth more than theirs, and that only more killing would bring about certain victory. Simply put: It is wrong to kill, it is especially wrong to kill the defenseless, and it is an abdication of the Bill of Rights to kill without due process of law." Later in his letter, Hale printed at the bottom of a page: "Best rule: to prevent terror on us we must stop the terror on them."

At the end of the letter, Hale wrote:

It would appear that I am here today to answer for the crime of stealing papers. For which I expect to spend some portion of my life in prison. But what I am really here for is having stolen something that which was never mine to take: precious human life. For which I was well-compensated and given a medal. My consequential decision to share classified information about the drone program with the public was a gesture not taken lightly, nor one I would have taken at all if I believed such a decision had the possibility of harming anyone but myself. I acted not for the sake of self-aggrandizement but that I might some day humbly ask forgiveness: So please, I beg, Forgive me, your honor, for the taking of papers as opposed to the lives of others. I could not, God so help me, have done otherwise.[38]

CHAPTER FOUR

MEDIA BOUNDARIES

NOT UNLIKE SQUADRONS OF MILITARY JETS, THE U.S.
media's war coverage flies information in formation. Notable departures from the pattern are few and far between; in general, the bigger the media outlet, the less likely the departure. While attending to collegial relations and professional reputations as well as adhering to understood missions, the employees of news organizations must comply with orders. The trajectories of individual careers might depend on many factors, but failure to sufficiently conform will knock a journalist's ascending career off course.

And so it was with Ashleigh Banfield.

For quite a while, the career of newswoman Ashleigh Banfield seemed damn near picture-perfect. After a dozen years of reporting for Canadian and U.S. television stations while winning numerous awards including an Emmy, in her early thirties she moved on to a big job at MSNBC in 2000 and was soon anchoring a prime-time show. Still rising, Banfield became a high-profile NBC News correspondent. The accolades for her work on cable and broadcast news were profuse. "Ms. Banfield, though somewhat informal in her delivery, fit nicely with MSNBC's positioning as the news network of choice for younger viewers," the *New York Times* explained. "Executives later admitted they also liked her frosted blond hair and trademark Clark Kent–style glasses. Just a few months after arriving at the network, she won raves from television critics for her coverage of the 2000 presidential election dispute. She approached it with a chatty style that MSNBC portrayed as a new journalistic approach."[1] Before long, Banfield was being touted as a potential heir to the NBC anchor chair occupied by Katie Couric.

Soon after 9/11, which she covered on camera just a few blocks from the World Trade Center while the North Tower fell, Banfield went to war zones; during the early autumn of 2001, she was in Afghanistan and Pakistan, then went on to report from seven Middle Eastern countries including Iraq, Iran, and Saudi Arabia.[2] "She's the age of the audience that we want and she's a great communicator," MSNBC president Erik Sorenson said in late October. "And I think she communicates in the authoritative, energetic way that this generation wants to be communicated to in."[3] The *Times* reported, "Ms. Banfield is widely considered within NBC News to be unusually gifted in front of a camera, with the sort of confidence and genuine delivery that is shared by an elite few in television news."[4]

But Banfield's career hit a wall as soon as she gave a speech at Kansas State University on April 24, 2003, two weeks after the fall of the big Saddam Hussein statue in Baghdad's Firdos Square. The speech "deeply offended many at NBC News," the *New York Times* recounted; it "was considered a major setback."[5]

In the midst of the United States' triumphalism about victory in Iraq, Ashleigh Banfield had dared to say this about U.S. media coverage:

> What didn't you see? You didn't see where those bullets landed. You didn't see what happened when the mortar landed. A puff of smoke is not what a mortar looks like when it explodes, believe me. There are horrors that were completely left out of this war. So was this journalism or was this coverage? There is a grand difference between journalism and coverage, and getting access does not mean you're getting the story, it just means you're getting one more arm or leg of the story. And that's what we got, and it was a glorious, wonderful picture that had a lot of people watching and a lot of advertisers excited about cable news. But it wasn't journalism, because I'm not so sure that we in America are hesitant to do this again, to fight another war, because it looked like a glorious and courageous and so successful terrific endeavor, and we got rid of a horrible leader: We got rid of a dictator, we got rid of a monster, but we didn't see what it took to do that.[6]

NBC responded quickly, saying: "Ms. Banfield does not speak for NBC News. We are deeply disappointed and troubled by her remarks, and will review her comments with her."[7] The network's management declared: "She and we both agreed that she didn't intend to demean the work of her colleagues, and she will choose her words more carefully in the future."[8]

Banfield's candor on a campus in Manhattan, Kansas, had infuriated the network's top bosses at 30 Rock in midtown

Manhattan, and her fall from corporate-media grace was swift. Six years later, she described what happened:

> I was office-less for ten months. No phone, no computer. For ten months I had to report to work every day and ask where I could sit. If somebody was away I could use their desk. Eventually, after ten months of this, I was given an office that was a tape closet. They cleared the tapes out and put a desk and a TV in there, and a computer and phone. It was pretty blatant. The message was crystal clear. Yet they wouldn't let me leave. I begged for seventeen months to be let out of my contract. If they had no use for me, let's just part ways amicably—no need for payouts, just a clean break. And Neal [Shapiro, the president of NBC] wouldn't allow it. I don't know what his rationale was—perhaps he thought I would take what I felt was a very strong brand, and others felt was a very strong brand, to another network and make a success of it. Maybe that's why he chose to keep me in a warehouse. I will never forgive him for his cruelty and the manner in which he decided to dispose of me.[9]

MORE THAN A FEW JOURNALISTS have struggled with how getting and telling the story can become thrilling and numbing at the same time. Even top-flight reporters are susceptible. One of the most noteworthy U.S. journalists of the twentieth century, I.F. Stone, acknowledged the hazard that "you forget what you are writing about. . . . [Y]ou are like a journalistic Nero fiddling while Rome burns and having a hell of a good time or like a small boy covering a hell of a big fire. It's just wonderful and exciting. You are a cub reporter and God has given you big fire to cover. And you forget, you forget it is really burning."[10]

Stone could have added that in the case of coverage related to war, it's easy to forget that people are really burning. We're led down garden paths of such forgetfulness while watching shows that originate from hot-lit cable TV studios, or reading the ponderous political columns in influential media outlets, or hearing the interviews with policy makers, think-tank experts, and standard authorities on how the United States should work its will on the world. In matters of war and peace, news media perform such crucial functions that they often resemble a fourth branch of government.

U.S. MEDIA SUPPORT FOR the "war on terror" has been as perpetual as the "war on terror" itself.

The goal of maximizing U.S. power projection is not controversial in relations between press and state. Despite tensions that can flare up between media and the Pentagon, the overall harmonies of reporting news and making war have endured, without a serious breach, for upwards of five decades. At times, high-profile journalists and top war architects might seem to be arm wrestling, but one hand is washing the other.

Along the way, war's victims can be scripted as mere extras in media dramas. During the fall of 2001, overwhelming media enthusiasm for attacking Afghanistan was never in doubt. And as the invasion of Iraq drew near, the mainstream media had less and less use for naysaying. Only many years and uncounted deaths later did the media vocabulary for those wars widen to include words like *mistake, blunder, hubris, miscalculation.* But to probe too deeply and illuminate the human suffering—and to directly connect it to those "mistakes" and "blunders"—would be too much of a threat to business as usual, for careers and for media institutions.

As with any politician, an individual journalist is potentially expendable (as sexual predators like NBC's Matt Lauer and Charlie Rose of CBS and PBS could ultimately attest). But, like the Pentagon and the CIA, multibillion-dollar media conglomerates will endure. The business of war and the business of news are thoroughly intertwined, and—no matter what political churn or corporate consolidation occurs—the essence of a military-industrial-media complex is structured to be resolute in retaining and wielding its power. The victims of war do not enter into the bottom line, and cognitive dissonance is not welcome as a disrupter.

In U.S. media coverage of U.S. wars, the patterns are far worse than checkered. Yet, without a doubt, notable exceptions to the dismal patterns do exist; occasionally, tough independent-minded reporting via a sizable media outlet does challenge the nation's war establishment. But the impacts of propaganda are not undermined by exceptional departures from the usual boundaries, which are professionally well understood—or at least heeded—even if internalized to the point of unconsciousness. "Circus dogs jump when the trainer cracks his whip," George Orwell observed, "but the really well-trained dog is the one that turns his somersault when there is no whip."[11]

Foreign correspondent Reese Erlich, with whom I traveled to Baghdad in September 2002, wrote a few weeks after our trip:

Most journalists who get plum foreign assignments already accept the assumptions of empire. I didn't meet a single foreign reporter in Iraq who disagreed with the notion that the U.S. and Britain have the right to overthrow the Iraqi government by force. They disagreed only about timing, whether the action should be unilateral, and whether a long-term occupation is practical. . . . When I raise the issue of sovereignty in casual conversation with my fellow scribes, they look as if I've arrived from Mars. Of course the U.S. has the right to overthrow Saddam Hussein, they argue, because he has weapons of mass destruction and might be a future threat to other countries. The implicit assumption is that the U.S.—as the world's sole superpower—has the right to make this decision. The U.S. must take the responsibility to remove unfriendly dictatorships and install friendly ones.

Erlich offered this assessment: "The U.S. is supposed to have the best and freest media in the world, but in my experience, having reported from dozens of countries, the higher up you go in the journalistic feeding chain, the less free the reporting."[12]

While covering warfare in Iraq, foreign correspondents routinely assumed the validity of the U.S. war effort, while in-studio anchors and commentators—including journalists at media outlets like the *New York Times* and *Washington Post* often invited onto the air—took as a given the good intentions of U.S. policy makers, whatever their policy failures. The bassline of media coverage was usually in tune with what often turned out to be specious predictions, if not bloviating falsehoods, coming from government functionaries, who ranged from lowly "public information officers" at the Pentagon to the commander in chief.

AS THE IRAQ WAR went on, disillusionment filtered into much of U.S. media, while outlets dodged their pivotal roles. The ten-year anniversary of the invasion was an occasion for the *New Yorker* to publish a retrospective article focusing on its own coverage of the war. Headlined "The Iraq War in The New Yorker," the piece had a tone of disappointed hopes, not surprising since the *New Yorker* had strongly supported the invasion during many months leading up to it. Now, in mid-March of 2013, the piece by the magazine's "ideas editor" asserted that "Americans, on the whole, regarded the war from a distance that wasn't merely physical but mental, emotional, even moral." (Near the article's beginning was a quoted snippet of prose from George Packer, one of the magazine's many writers who'd been enthusiastic about the virtues of invading Iraq and making war there; he wrote in 2005 that, for Americans, "Iraq was a strangely distant war. It was always hard to picture the place; the war didn't enter the popular imagination in songs that everyone soon knew by heart, in the manner of previous wars.") "Before the war started," the magazine's ten-year overview went on, "it had seemed fairly comprehensible: the goal was to topple Saddam, find his weapons, and leave a more democratic government behind. But in the days, months, and years after the fall of Baghdad, the Iraq War became extraordinarily complicated and obscure."[13]

If you were reading the piece for a wisp of self-criticism

or even introspection from a publication that had championed the invasion, you would have been disappointed. On the contrary, the main mission of the 2,200-word piece seemed to involve touting the magazine's consistent high quality and providing many examples of the excellent articles that had been published "as *The New Yorker* tried to make sense of the war." Along the way, the retrospective devoted one sentence to a seminal piece that had appeared before the invasion: "Many people wrestled with the question of whether or not to go to war—including *The New Yorker*'s editor, David Remnick, in a February 3, 2003, Comment called 'Making a Case.'"

It's not hard to see why the magazine's retrospection without introspection would quickly glide past the "Making a Case" article without lingering at all. Remnick was still the *New Yorker* editor (as he would continue to be throughout the 2010s and beyond). His piece had reached readers on January 26—as it turned out, fifty-two days before the invasion of Iraq began. In the concluding section of his de facto editorial for the magazine, he wrote that the UN inspection team then doing its work in Iraq was not likely to be able to provide "irrefutable evidence that an enemy is amassing weapons of mass destruction." After all, Remnick added, "the Iraqis are highly experienced in the craft of 'cheat and retreat.'" His article concluded: "History will not easily excuse us if, by deciding not to decide, we defer a reckoning with an aggressive totalitarian leader who intends not only to develop weapons of mass destruction but also to use them. Saddam's abdication, or a military coup, would be a godsend; his sudden conversion to the wisdom of disarmament almost as good. It is a fine thing to dream. But, assuming such dreams are not realized, a return to a hollow pursuit of containment will be the most dangerous option of all."[14]

The *New Yorker* editor's clarion call for the United States to invade Iraq was a strong note in an orchestrated push for war. Remnick played his part not only with his writing but also, more importantly, with the power he exercised to showcase articles vehemently favoring an invasion—including pieces promoting false claims of ties between Saddam Hussein and al Qaeda[15]—in his influential magazine.[16]

The horrors that began with the Iraq invasion ended up eliciting little more than the equivalents of shrugs from media powerhouses about the professionals in their ranks who had greased the skids for the invasion to happen in the first place, while sounding alarms about the existence of Iraqi weapons of mass destruction that turned out not to exist. For the *New Yorker*, the *New York Times*, the *Washington Post*, and many other major outlets that had backed the invasion via slanted reporting and prominent commentaries, the disasters they had helped to bring about became grist for countless stories from their journalistic mills. The same big media operations that had done the most to assist with agenda building to start the war were later the best positioned, with their resources and prestige, to dominate the wartime coverage as years went by. Meanwhile, those media outlets maintained almost complete silence about their own shameful roles that had fueled the drive to war. When the *Times* and the *Post* finally managed to publish pieces of self-criticism, they were badly understated and fleeting.[17]

The capacity of large media institutions to evade any accountability for the carnage and anguish they helped to cause is akin to throwing unpleasant truths down a memory hole and turning out the lights. The same sort of conformity that was so pernicious during the run-up to the Iraq invasion has been replicated since then. Remaining silent about their culpability, powerful media outlets keep imparting tacit messages about the relative unimportance of the war victims: if eminent journalists and news organizations are able to skate past their record of support for Washington's calamitous war agendas, how really important could the lives lost and damaged—and the lives continuing to be lost and damaged—actually be?

TEN YEARS AFTER CALLING the Iraq War "one of the noblest things this country has ever attempted abroad," *New York Times* columnist Thomas Friedman was careful to dodge the fact that he'd supported the war from the outset.[18] The denial was more than just an effort to cover reputational tracks; it also reflected a standard attitude among media and policy elites, rarely stated aloud yet pervasive, as if helping to usher in U.S. wars was a no-fault undertaking, reasonably forgettable if need be. With such privileges looming large, the lives of people trapped in war would seem small.

There had been nothing equivocal about Friedman's response on May 30, 2003—ten weeks after the Iraq invasion began—when he appeared on the PBS program hosted by Charlie Rose, who began by noting that "people had criticisms about going in" and then asked: "Was it worth doing?"

"Oh, I think it was unquestionably worth doing," Friedman replied. Then he praised the war in Iraq as necessary to counter a "terrorism bubble," citing 9/11 along the way (despite the absence of a connection between Iraq's government and al Qaeda). "What we needed to do was go over to that part of the world, I'm afraid, and burst that bubble. We needed to go over there basically and take out a very big stick right in the heart of that world and burst that bubble." Friedman went on: "What they needed to see was American boys and girls going house to house from Basra to Baghdad and basically saying, 'Which part of this sentence don't you understand? You don't think, you know, we care about our open society? You think this bubble fantasy, we're just going to let it grow? Well, *suck on this.*' That, Charlie, was what this war was about. We could have hit Saudi Arabia. It was part of that bubble. Could have hit Pakistan. We hit Iraq because we could. That's the real truth."[19]

But in mid-2013, when Friedman discussed the Iraq War on NPR affiliate KQED Radio in San Francisco, he made no mention of his early support for the war. So I phoned in and spoke on the air, saying that there was a "dire shortage of remorse, particularly given Thomas Friedman's very large role in cheering on, with his usual caveats, but cheering on the invasion of Iraq before it took place." Friedman responded: "Well first of all, I would invite, I wrote a book called *Longitudes and Attitudes* that has all my columns leading up to the Iraq War. And what you'll find if you read those columns is someone agonizing over a very very difficult decision."[20]

TO ASSESS THE IMPLICIT as well as explicit messaging to the American public about the value of certain human lives, it's important to scrutinize not only the content of news coverage and punditry, but also the entertainment for mass audiences.

Released on Christmas Day, *American Sniper* became 2014's top-grossing film with a domestic box office of $350 million.[21] Later, when the chief movie critics of the *New York Times* teamed up to name "the ten most influential films" of the decade, *American Sniper* was at the top of the list. "With its pro-military, pro-gun flag waving—and fallen-warrior protagonist—*American Sniper* showed which way the political winds were howling," the critics wrote.[22] Yet the film's director, Clint Eastwood, demurred when an interviewer asked whether the film glorified war. "I think it's nice for veterans, because it shows what they go through, and that life—and the wives and families of veterans," he replied. "It was a great indication of the stresses they are under." Eastwood claimed that the film actually had "kind of an antiwar" message.[23]

The man who wrote the movie's script, Jason Hall, said he was drawn to the project of dramatizing the real-life Navy SEAL sniper Chris Kyle after learning that Kyle was the most lethal sniper in U.S. military history. The hero had gained renown during several tours in Iraq. For the scriptwriter, telling his story would be vitally revealing because the time had come "that we understand the sacrifice of these warriors. We didn't set out to explore the archetype of war; we set out to explore the archetype of the warrior. We did that from one man's point of view."[24]

American Sniper made sense to so many people by remaining in close proximity to the nation's media and political baselines. An essay by Pulitzer Prize–winning novelist Viet Thanh Nguyen addressed such dynamics in the context of an earlier American war. "All wars are fought twice, the first time on the battlefield, the second time in memory," he wrote.

This is certainly true for what Americans call the "Vietnam War" and what the victorious Vietnamese call the "American War." Both terms obscure how a war that killed more than 58,000 Americans and three million Vietnamese was also fought in Laos and Cambodia, killing hundreds of thousands more and leading directly to the Cambodian genocide. In its own typically solipsistic, American-centered, whitewashed fashion, Hollywood has been waging this war on celluloid ever since John Wayne's atrocious *Green Berets* in 1968, a film so nakedly propagandistic it could have been made by the Third Reich.[25]

Nguyen added: "Born in Vietnam but made in America, I have a personal and professional interest in Hollywood's fetish about this war. Unfortunately, I have watched almost every 'Vietnam War' movie that Hollywood has made. It's an exercise I recommend to no one." And, he observed, "a war story that repeats a purely American point of view will just help ensure that American wars continue, only with more diverse American soldiers and ever-newer targets to be killed or saved. What kind of war story sees through the other's point of view, hears her questions, takes seriously her assessment of ourselves? Would it even be a war story? And isn't that the story we should tell?"[26]

"IT IS THE INNOCENCE which constitutes the crime," James Baldwin wrote.[27]

Innocence must be stubborn in the midst of the warfare state. As time goes on, incriminating designs emerge. They can be seen as system failures that undermine good intentions—or as systemic priorities that yield predictably cruel, even barbaric, results. In mainstream media, even the best reporting is oriented to assume that Washington's war policy makers, whatever their flaws, have creditable goals.

Consider how the *New York Times* framed a laudable blockbuster scoop near the end of 2021, drawing on some 1,300 confidential documents.[28] Under the big headline "Hidden Pentagon Records Reveal Patterns of Failure in Deadly Airstrikes," the *Times* assessed U.S. bombing in Iraq, Syria, and Afghanistan—and reported that "since 2014, the American air war has been plagued by deeply flawed intelligence, rushed and imprecise targeting and the deaths of thousands of civilians, many of them children."[29] Bold-type words like "failure," "flawed intelligence," and "imprecise targeting" were apt to obscure the inconvenient truth that virtually none of it was unforeseeable; the killings had resulted from policies that gave very low priority to prevention of civilian deaths. The gruesome record was not so much a matter of incompetence as a premeditated policy with expectable results—considered to be quite acceptable.

FOR U.S. MEDIA, during twenty years, the Afghanistan Story was overwhelmingly the American Story. People living in the country were, in effect, relegated to roles of bit players in a drama with a narrative featuring efforts by Americans to do good under dangerous conditions. When the last U.S. troops left Afghanistan, the Security Policy Reform Institute astutely concluded that "the degree of violence experienced by Afghan civilians has never driven U.S. media coverage, particularly when the U.S. itself has been directly or indirectly responsible."[30]

Except for three time spans—the American invasion, the surge of troops sent in by Obama early in his presidency, and the withdrawal—the level of attention to Afghanistan was notably low on the nightly newscasts from ABC, CBS, and NBC, barometers of mainstream coverage and by far the most pervasive sources of TV news for Americans. Citing figures from the authoritative *Tyndall Report*, the institute pointed out that "national news coverage of Afghanistan by the three major networks totaled just five minutes across the 14,000 minutes of evening news broadcasts in 2020, and only 362 from all of the 2015–2019 period. In total: coverage of Afghanistan amounted to an average of twenty-four minutes per network, per year, for a conflict on which the U.S. has spent $2.3 trillion of the public's funds."

During the two decades, until the dramatic full departure, the quantity of news airtime was in sync with American boots on Afghan soil. "Following the initial stages of the U.S. invasion, television coverage roughly tracked with the number of U.S. troops deployed to Afghanistan," the institute noted. "Coverage picked up again during the U.S. troop surge in 2009 and reached its third-highest point in terms of minutes allotted when there were around 90,000 troops in Afghanistan in 2010. When U.S. troop levels in Afghanistan dropped, so did network coverage. The violence didn't go away when U.S. troops started to leave Afghanistan, but major media networks did."

To television producers in the United States, continuation of the USA's air war in Afghanistan was hardly newsworthy. Andrew Tyndall, an expert researcher of TV news content, summed up: "For the American networks, 'war' means troops on the ground in harm's way, not use of lethal force remotely by the Pentagon."[31]

WHEN PRESIDENT BIDEN PULLED the last U.S. troops out of Afghanistan in late August 2021, the reaction from corporate media was often negative for reasons quite apart from how ineptly the withdrawal took place. While polls were showing that most Americans favored the decision to pull out, the response from prestigious reporters and pundits was frequently the opposite. Researchers at Fairness and Accuracy In Reporting studied the intense week of TV evening news coverage by ABC, CBS, and NBC—with a combined nightly viewership of 20 million—beginning when the Taliban took control of Kabul; the seventy-four sources on the air were heavily weighted against the withdrawal. "No scholars or antiwar activists from either the U.S. or Afghanistan were featured," media analyst Julie Hollar found, while "only two civil society leaders made appearances." As for the wisdom of ending the U.S. war effort in Afghanistan after twenty years of fighting there, "Biden, who played a key role in leading the country into the Iraq War, was essentially the strongest 'antiwar' voice in the conversation. While he and his administration frequently defended their decision to uphold the withdrawal agreement, there were no other sources who did so."[32]

For their part, eminent network correspondents could not resist editorializing to viewers in the guise of reporting at a historic juncture. Chief NBC foreign correspondent Richard Engel opined: "A twenty-year war, the longest in U.S. history, today ended in disgrace. The U.S. leaving behind a country its citizens are too terrified to live in."[33] Implicitly, the "disgrace" was not the U.S. war effort but its end.

From *CBS Evening News* anchor Norah O'Donnell came an assessment solemnly prefaced with this opening: "We wanted to take a moment to reflect on what we're seeing in Afghanistan as we end America's longest war." She went on, "When America leaves, for many, so does the hope—the hope of freedom, the hope for human rights. And in its place comes the sheer terror of what's next." And, from the network's Manhattan studios, O'Donnell said: "Wars are costly to start and costly to end. It's costly to stay and costly to leave. The cost in lives—the nearly 2,500 American troops lost, the families they left behind. And the more than 20,000 wounded warriors, some wondering: were our sacrifices worth it?"[34]

While summing up "America's longest war," the CBS anchor did not say a single word to indicate that "the cost in lives" included any Afghan people.

FOR AMERICAN TELEVISION NETWORKS, "what was newsworthy was the fall of Kabul and the pullout of U.S. troops, not the fate of the Afghan people in the aftermath," said Tyndall, whose *Tyndall Report* monitors the biggest networks' evening news shows.[35] Journalist Jim Lobe, who'd been covering U.S. foreign policy for four decades, wrote a few days before 2022 began, "Despite unprecedented levels of hunger and starvation for which U.S. sanctions bear important responsibility, Afghanistan has once again virtually disappeared from the most important single source of world news for most Americans. Since September, which marked the end of U.S. efforts to evacuate its citizens and its foreign and

Afghan allies, the evening news programs of the three domi-nant U.S. television networks—ABC, NBC, and CBS—have collectively devoted a grand total of twenty-one minutes—spread over ten story segments—to Afghanistan."[36]

Some exceptions provided coverage of the Afghan famine emergency, such as a piece that aired on the widely watched CBS program *60 Minutes*. But, symptomatically, even that exceptional reporting let the U.S. government off the hook, as Lobe noted: "What was missing in the *60 Minutes* seg-ment, as with the two evening news segments about the crisis on ABC and NBC, however, was any focus on the U.S. role in restricting or blocking funding that could help alleviate its catastrophic impact."[37]

At Fairness and Accuracy In Reporting, Julie Hollar wrote that "as the United States withdrew militarily from Afghanistan in August, U.S. TV news interest in the plight of the country's citizens spiked, often focusing on 'the horror awaiting women and girls' to argue against withdrawal. Four months later, as those same citizens have been plunged into a humanitarian crisis due in no small part to U.S. sanctions, where is the outrage?"[38]

After twenty years of American military intervention, often justified in the name of assisting the Afghan people, the worsening disaster received little attention from U.S. media overall. The meager coverage that did happen typically lacked clear context—which could have put a spotlight on Washing-ton to take urgent action. "The Taliban shoulder some blame, having banned women from most paid jobs outside of teach-ing and health care, costing the economy up to 5 percent of its GDP," Hollar noted, but "a much bigger driver of the crisis has been the U.S.-led sanctions on the Taliban."

During the first months of 2022, the situation worsened in Afghanistan. Severe malnutrition was widespread. As spring began, Human Rights Watch cited an estimate that upwards of thirteen thousand newborn babies in the country—one in ten—had died since January.[39] More than three million Afghan children urgently needed nutritional support. But major news outlets in the United States weren't paying attention. Like the Pentagon, the American media establishment had moved on, and Afghan people could fade to black.

SPEAKING AT THE UNITED NATIONS in the autumn of 2021, President Biden proclaimed: "I stand here today, for the first time in twenty years, with the United States not at war. We've turned the page."[40] But actually, the "turned" page was bound into a continuing volume of war. Biden's claim was mendacious, on a global scale. In September, the same month as his pronouncement at the UN, a new report from the Costs of War Project at Brown University showed that the "war on terror" was still underway on several continents. The project's co-director Professor Catherine Lutz said that "the war continues in over eighty countries." The documentation was clear: "counterterrorism operations have become more widespread in recent years."[41]

For news media, the president's declaration that the United States was "not at war" helped to inch ongoing warfare into a different category, as if war wasn't really war anymore. (When the White House released Biden's 2023 military budget request six months later, Reuters flatly reported that it would be a record "peacetime" budget.[42]) News coverage had already been headed in that direction anyway; over the many years, U.S. war had gotten old, not much more notable than background noise. The USA's mere engagement in some kind of warfare somewhere or other became less and less likely to rise above the level of a dog-bites-man story. And a key truth is that very few journalists reporting for Americans know a lot about what their military is actually doing in, say, Africa or the Philippines[43] or remote areas of Syria—and what they do know, or think they know, is mostly based on what official sources tell them. The results are commonly much more stenographic than journalistic.[44] When handed a narration with presumed facts to relay, journalists on deadline are well positioned to tell readers, listeners, and viewers the official story.

CHAPTER FIVE

"HUMANE" WARS

This is what American troops were doing before terrorists struck today: feeding children, playing with kids, lending an arm to the elderly. The American military is the greatest in the world, not only because of its superior force, but because of its humanity—soldiers providing a helping hand, pulling Afghan infants to safety. This child kept warm by the uniform of a U.S. soldier during her evacuation. This mother delivered her baby in the cargo bay of a C-17, naming the newborn Reach, after the call sign of the aircraft that rescued her.

For the last two decades, our mission has been about keeping us safe at home and improving the lives of Afghans. The thirteen U.S. service members who made the ultimate sacrifice today did not die in vain. One hundred thousand people have been evacuated because of their heroic actions. They answered the call and did what they were trained to do. A reminder of the high price of freedom. And God bless our U.S. troops.

—*CBS EVENING NEWS* ANCHOR
NORAH O'DONNELL, AUGUST 6, 2021[1]

THE PHYSICAL AND PSYCHOLOGICAL DISTANCES OF HIGH-
tech killing have encouraged belief in frequent claims that
American warfare has become humane.[2] Such pretenses
should be grimly absurd to anyone who has read high-quality
journalism from eyewitness reporters like Anand Gopal. For
instance, his article for the *New Yorker* in September 2021,
"The Other Afghan Women," was an in-depth, devastating
piece that exposed the slaughter and terror systematically
inflicted on rural residents of Afghanistan by the U.S. Air
Force.[3] Gopal, who worked in Afghanistan for several years
while often going to remote areas, brought into focus lives
usually relegated to U.S. media's unseen shadows.

Civilian deaths were "grossly undercounted" during the
twenty-year U.S. war in Afghanistan, Gopal said during an
interview on *Democracy Now!* soon after the withdrawal of
U.S. troops from the country.[4] With 70 percent of the Afghan
population living in rural areas, Gopal was one of the few
reporters for U.S. outlets to spend a lot of time there—particularly in such places as the large Helmand Province in southern Afghanistan, "really the epicenter of the violence for the
last two decades." Gopal spoke of a housewife named Shakira, living in the small village of Pan Killay in Sangin Valley:
"I had the opportunity to meet her and interview her a number
of times. And, you know, I'm somebody who's been covering
this conflict for many years, and even I was taken aback by the
sheer level of violence that people like her had gone through and
had witnessed."

Gopal learned that Shakira had lost sixteen members of her
family. And the context was stunning:

What was remarkable or astonishing about this was that this wasn't in one airstrike or in one mass casualty incident. This was in fourteen or fifteen different incidents over twenty years. So, there was one cousin who was carrying a hot plate for cooking, and that hot plate was mistaken for an IED, a roadside bomb, and he was killed. There was another cousin who was a farmer, who was in the field and had encountered a coalition patrol, and he was shot dead. Shakira told me his body was just left there like an animal. So, there were so many different instances. So, people were living—reliving tragedy again and again. And it wasn't just Shakira, because I was interested, after interviewing her, to see how representative this was. So, I managed to talk to over a dozen families. I got the names of the people who were killed. I tried to triangulate that information with death certificates and other eyewitnesses. And so, the level of human loss is really extraordinary. And most of these deaths were never recorded. It's usually the big airstrikes that make the media, because in these areas there's not a lot of internet penetration, there's not—there's no media there. And so, a lot of the smaller deaths of ones and twos don't get recorded. And so, I think we've grossly undercounted the number of civilians who died in this war.[5]

While some independent organizations have devoted themselves to collecting figures on civilian deaths, the U.S. government is not oriented toward counting such numbers. Overall, civilian anonymity cuts against accountability. At the same time, best estimates place the proportion of civilian deaths in recent decades at between 75 and 90 percent of all war deaths.[6] With extremely rare exceptions, the people killed and maimed by the U.S. military aren't on American screens or in print, their names are unknown, their lives remain a blank of un-personhood. In aggregate, those lives must remain impersonal and insignificant if war efforts are to go on unimpeded. By dint of repetition compulsion, with virtual distancing in a hyperdigital era, making war has taken on a life, and death, of its own; doing more than just blending in with the everyday, the normalized fatal violence disappears from view for all who are insulated from its cruelties, "normal" and unremarkable.

IN THE LATE SUMMER OF 2021, Yale professor Samuel Moyn made a splash with *Humane: How the United States Abandoned Peace and Reinvented War.* The new book was well documented on legal issues related to war, and the author provided thoughtful analysis of some antiwar efforts from the nineteenth century to the present. But even while warning that U.S. warfare since 9/11 was set to be perpetual, he asserted that it had become "humane." In the process, the book repeatedly made assertions that would seem preposterous to people living in Iraq or Afghanistan.

In an opinion piece that the *New York Times* printed when his book came out, shortly after United States forces left Afghanistan, Moyn wrote flatly: "With the last American troops now out of the country, it is clearer what America's bequest to the world has been over the past twenty years: a disturbing new form of counterterrorist belligerency, at once endless and humane. This has transformed American traditions of war-making, and the withdrawal from Afghanistan is, in fact, a final step in the transformation."[7]

For all his sophistication and nuanced analysis, Moyn's outlook is typical of insulation from human realities of war. Seemingly complacent about those realities in the present day, he accepts the chronic discounting and undercounting of deaths and injuries from recent and ongoing U.S. warfare. And Moyn bypasses the longer-term effects of the United States' twenty-first-century wars—including the decimation of entire societies and nations; the cascading results of all the killing, the maiming, and the crushing of infrastructure from health care to education to housing; the ecological destruction; the spiritual desecration; the terror imposed on daily life for years on end.

Such terror includes knowing that the sound of an approaching drone could mean imminent death. Yet one can read in *Humane* that "for all their faults, it is also true that drones are increasingly the cleanest mode of war ever conceived. They hover nearby and, when they attack, do so with painstaking real-time targeting in the name of precision and thus civilian care."[8] And: "The American way of war is more and more defined by a near complete immunity from harm for one side and unprecedented care when it comes to killing people on the other."[9] Overall, Moyn fuels a pernicious myth that U.S. wars can now be understood as somehow close to benign, even while he knows and occasionally notes otherwise. The professor ends up grading U.S. wars on a curve, giving them increasingly high marks the farther they are from the carnage in Southeast Asia during the 1960s and 1970s.

✧

FROM VIETNAM TO AFGHANISTAN, the official pretense from the commander in chief was that America's brave troops—imbued with the nation's highest ideals—were on a humane mission.

"No American army in all of our long history has ever been so compassionate," President Lyndon Johnson told thousands of troops who assembled to hear him at Cam Ranh Bay in Vietnam on October 26, 1966.[10] Nearly fifty years later, the themes of President Barack Obama's oratory to troops in Afghanistan were strikingly similar. In fact, both of those presidents could have delivered the bulk of each other's speeches without changing a word.

"The troops" as a single entity have been useful in many a political story. It's not necessary to question the sincerity of a politician who heaps reverent praise on the troops to recognize that men and women in military service are often invoked to personify the pursuit of war policies that they had no role whatsoever in devising or approving; they are not partners but props and pawns for Washington's officialdom, which uses them in public relations dramas and battles over policy as war drags on. And, as with Johnson's "compassionate" claim, officials often strive to depict the troops as angels of mercy rather than killers.

Historian Victor Brooks described the scene at Cam Ranh Bay, the first time a president had gone to a war zone in more than twenty years, which became a prototype for future commanders in chief: "Johnson, dressed in his action-oriented 'ranch/country' attire of tan slacks and a matching field jacket embossed with the gold seal of the American presidency, emerged from the plane with the demeanor of a man seeking to test his mettle in a saloon gunfight. Standing in the rear of an open Jeep, the president clutched a handrail and received the cheers of seven thousand servicemen and the rattle of musketry down a line of a nine-hundred-man honor guard." In his speech, Johnson "compared the sweating suntanned men in olive drab fatigues to their predecessors at Valley Forge, Gettysburg, Iwo Jima, and Pusan. He insisted that they would be remembered long after by 'a grateful public of a grateful nation.'"[11] At that point, 325,000 American soldiers were already on the ground in Vietnam, and many more were to come.[12]

Addressing his oratory to "my fellow Americans, soldiers, sailors, airmen, and marines," Johnson praised them to the skies and let them know that the war's top U.S. general, William Westmoreland, had told him that "no armed forces anywhere, at any time, commanded by any commander in chief, were up to the group that we have in Vietnam now." Johnson added, "I cannot decorate each of you, but I cannot visualize a better decoration for any of you to have than to know that this great soldier thinks that you are the best prepared, that you are the most skilled, that you know what you are doing, and you know why you are doing it—and you are doing it."[13]

Barack Obama was just five years old when Johnson spoke, yet the continuity between their speeches in Vietnam and Afghanistan would end up being almost seamless. They were basically saying the same thing to the troops—you are great, keep fighting, the folks back home are proud of you, and they profoundly appreciate your noble sacrifices to protect the lives of the innocent. The momentum of such adulation easily leads to the idea that America's troops engage in warfare with exemplary benevolence.

✦

ON MARCH 28, 2010, Barack Obama made his first presidential trip to Afghanistan. The visit was a surprise, adding to the dramatic impact. Minutes before airing Obama's speech live from Bagram Air Base, CNN reported that "he will be meeting with U.S. troops there," and the network's anchor added:

> Always an exciting visit when the president meets troops, especially in a war-torn area. This Afghanistan war going now into its eighth year, and there had been a lot of angst expressed by some U.S. troops, according to some of our reporting from Barbara Starr, Pentagon correspondent, that many troops were kind of feeling like when is the president going to be visiting us here in Afghanistan. And this is kind of a real shot in the arm in terms of boosting morale to see the commander in chief there in Afghanistan, and visiting face to face with the U.S. troops.[14]

The anchor's setup was revealing. To hear the network tell it, the "angst expressed" by U.S. troops involved their unrequited eagerness to be visited by the president. There was no mention of angst related to the death, injuries, grief, fear, and destruction in their midst.

Awaiting Obama's arrival at the podium, CNN's White House correspondent Dan Lothian provided some numbers on the U.S. escalation in Afghanistan: "And so the troop ramp-up, as one official said, has reached about 80,000, expected to get to 100,000."[15] Soon, speaking to two thousand assembled troops, Obama took a deep dive into exaggeration and flattery. "I want you to know that everybody back home is proud of you," he said. "Everybody back home is grateful. . . . And all of you represent the virtues and the values that America so desperately needs right now: sacrifice and selflessness, honor and decency. That's what I see here today. That's what you represent." Later came a theme of glory in selfless death: "I've been humbled by your sacrifice in the solemn homecoming of flag-draped coffins at Dover, to the headstones in section 60 at Arlington, where the fallen from this war rest in peace alongside the fellow heroes of America's story. So here in Afghanistan, each one of you is part of an unbroken line of American service members who have sacrificed for over two centuries."[16]

Two years later, Obama was back at Bagram Air Base. He gave an eleven-minute speech, which began by declaring that "here, in Afghanistan, more than half a million of our sons and daughters have sacrificed to protect our country." Of course he could not use phrases in disrepute such as "light at the end of the tunnel," but the implications of his oratory were the same. Whatever he might have actually believed, the president sounded upbeat. "Over the last three years, the tide has turned," he said. While acknowledging that "there will be difficult days ahead" and "the enormous sacrifices of our men and women are not over," he exuded confidence and proceeded to talk about "how we will complete our mission and end the war in Afghanistan."[17]

Perhaps no one could question Obama's sincerity when he said that "as president, nothing is more wrenching than signing a letter to a family of the fallen, or looking into the eyes of a child who will grow up without a mother or father."

And he certainly sounded high-minded: "Today, we recall the fallen and those who suffered wounds, both seen and unseen. But through dark days, we have drawn strength from their example and the ideals that have guided our nation and led the world—a belief that all people are treated equal and deserve the freedom to determine their destiny. That is the light that guides us still."[18]

But such guiding light would lead to ghastly results.

SITTING IN A WHEELCHAIR in January 2006, thirty-eight years after his combat duties suddenly ended on a Vietnam battlefield, Ron Kovic wrote a cri de coeur with questions that authorities and mass media showed no signs of wanting to really hear, much less answer, as the Iraq War neared the end of its third year: "Do the American people, the president, the politicians, senators and congressmen who sent us to this war have any idea what it really means to lose an arm or a leg, to be paralyzed, to begin to cope with the psychological wounds of that war? Do they have any concept of the long-term effects of these injuries, how the struggles of the wounded are only now just beginning?"

Kovic was living realities of war that were off the media maps, banished beyond the margins of teleprompters: "This is the part you never see. The part that is never reported in the news. The part that the president and vice president never mention. This is the agonizing part, the lonely part, when you have to awake to the wound each morning and suddenly realize what you've lost, what is gone forever. They're out there and they have mothers and fathers, sisters and brothers, husbands and wives and children. And they're not saying much right now. Just like me they're just trying to get through each day. Trying to be brave and not cry."[19]

As for people on the receiving end of the USA's military prowess—civilians or, even more objectified, the fallen among enemy forces—within American media they don't amount to much more than trees falling unseen and unheard in a forest. This generalization does not contradict the instances of high-quality, against-the-grain journalism that sometimes appears even in media outlets with wide reach. Yet, as discussed in Chapter 1, exceptional stories and commentaries are, well, exceptions. And the exceptions, while they can be quite valuable, are not the essence of propaganda. Repetition is.

News that discredits elite managers of the war system can startle and shake things up for a brief time, sending damage-control mechanisms into overdrive. It might seem that the status quo has been jerked away from its moorings. But such tempests blow over, leaving little changed. Sometimes, in the process, high-ranking officials get slapped on the wrist. They might even be tossed overboard.

After fulsome presidential praise as the new leader of U.S. armed forces in Afghanistan, two multistarred generals in succession—Stanley McChrystal and then David Petraeus—were hoisted onto clouds of media adulation before crashing to earth and losing their exalted positions. Those four-star heroes lost their pinnacle posts for reasons that had nothing to do with the deaths of civilians or anyone else during their commands.

McChrystal was a media darling from the moment he took charge of all U.S. forces in Afghanistan during the late spring of 2009. Hailed as bluntly outspoken, he also generated plenty of admiring stories about his spartan rigor. A *New*

York Times profile led off this way: "You have to marvel at how Lt. Gen. Stanley A. McChrystal, a former Special Operations commander and the newly appointed leader of American forces in Afghanistan, does it. Mastermind the hunt for al Qaeda in Iraq and plot stealth raids on Taliban strongholds in the Hindu Kush while getting just a few hours of sleep a night, exercising enough to exhaust a gym rat and eating one meal a day to avoid sluggishness. One meal. Who was it who said an army runs on its stomach?"[20] And so it went, with media gushing at General McChrystal's acetic stamina and tireless grit—till he stepped over an unacceptable line, not because he was overseeing a military force killing and terrorizing too many civilians, but because he said negative things to a *Rolling Stone* reporter about people in the Obama administration as high up as Vice President Joe Biden.

When the magazine quoted McChrystal's indiscreet comments in an article, Obama relieved the general of his command.[21] A dozen years later, when Obama's memoir appeared, the book clarified that the firing had taken place due to concern about McChrystal's display of "impunity." The former president explained this way: "[I]n that *Rolling Stone* article, I'd heard in him and his aides the same air of impunity that seemed to have taken hold among some of the military's top ranks during the Bush years: a sense that once the war began, those who fought it shouldn't be questioned, that politicians should just give them what they ask for and get out of the way. It was a seductive view, especially coming from a man of McChrystal's caliber. It also threatened to erode a bedrock principle of our representative democracy, and I was determined to put an end to it."[22]

To the president, the general's only unacceptable "air of

impunity" had to do with a lack of respect for America's dip-
lomats and elected leadership. The air of impunity from a
military commander toward Afghan lives was another matter
entirely.

ONE OF THE TERRIBLE REALITIES of wars after they're over is
that they aren't really over. Wars can end as far as media, politicians, and historians are concerned, but the cascading and
enduring effects are just getting started.

In the United States, real-time concerns "during Vietnam"
dissipated and faded after the last helicopter lifted off from
the roof of the U.S. embassy in Saigon. But the Vietnam that
continued to exist after dismissed from American concerns
was left to cope with awful legacies, among them unexploded
ordnances that continued to take Vietnamese lives. (Children
were apt to find explosive devices and mistake them for toys.)
Four decades after the war ended, citing a 2014 impact survey,
the Stimson Center pointed out that "unexploded bombs and
cluster munitions contaminate over 23,670 square miles"—
amounting to "19 percent of Vietnam's total land area."[23]
Vietnam and Laos were also left to cope with the long-term
effects of the U.S. military's massive use of the defoliant Agent
Orange that have included birth defects.[24]

America left Vietnam with an estimated three million dead,
huge numbers of injured and missing human beings, unspeak-
able destruction, and a horrendously ravaged ecology. But
the postwar presidential tone was set by Jimmy Carter two
months after taking office in early 1977. Asked at a news
conference if he felt "any moral obligation to help rebuild
that country," here's how President Carter replied: "Well, the

destruction was mutual. You know, we went to Vietnam without any desire to capture territory or to impose American will on other people. We went there to defend the freedom of the South Vietnamese. And I don't feel that we ought to apologize or to castigate ourselves or to assume the status of culpability."[25]

The U.S. veterans and their families who suffered from Agent Orange's severe health effects were up against policies of marginalization and denial from the Defense Department and the Veterans Administration. Veterans and their advocates had to fight for recognition and assistance: provided, if ever, only belatedly and inadequately.[26] For some, aid came too late.

Although research was less extensive, indications of similar patterns unfolded with depleted uranium (DU), which became part of the Pentagon's arsenal as hardened material for piercing enemy tanks and so forth. While bracing itself for the invasion that came in early 2003, Iraq was still coping with effects of the U.S. military's use of DU in 1991 during the Gulf War. "Something is very, very wrong in southern Iraq," my colleague Reese Erlich reported after our visit to Iraq in September 2002. "At Basra's Children's and Maternity Hospital, doctors display a large photo album of hundreds of children born with horrible birth defects. One study conducted by Iraqi doctors indicated that 0.776 percent of Basra-area children were born with birth defects in 1998, compared to just 0.304 percent in 1990, before the Gulf War. Another study showed a rise in childhood cancers and other malignancies of 384.2 percent from 1990–2000."[27] Despite such warning signs, the U.S. military proceeded to fire about 180,000 rounds of depleted uranium during the 2003 invasion.[28] Long afterward, as a 2020 article in the *Bulletin of the Atomic Scientists* noted, epidemiological research remained sparse.[29]

U.S. veterans who'd encountered high levels of DU received minimal attention or redress. In 2015, when the National Institutes of Health published a longitudinal study of thirty-five veterans who'd been exposed in "Iraqi conflicts," it concluded that "fragment retainment and related scarring was [*sic*] significantly increased in veterans exposed to high levels of DU."[30] And depleted uranium was just one concern.

Gulf War veterans were exposed to a warlock's brew of chemicals, burning oil, and many other biological insults. The 1991 conflict gave rise to the term "Gulf War syndrome." In 2010, the National Academy of Sciences announced findings that "military service in the Persian Gulf War is a cause of post-traumatic stress disorder in some veterans and is also associated with multi-symptom illness; gastrointestinal disorders such as irritable bowel syndrome; substance abuse, particularly alcoholism; and psychiatric problems such as anxiety disorder." The proportion of affected veterans was very high—"nearly 700,000 U.S. personnel were deployed to the region and more than 250,000 of them suffer from persistent, unexplained symptoms."[31]

As for wars of the twenty-first century, an extraordinary moment came on March 1, 2022, during President Biden's first State of the Union address. "Our troops in Iraq and Afghanistan faced many dangers," he said. "One was stationed at bases and breathing in toxic smoke from 'burn pits' that incinerated wastes of war—medical and hazard material, jet fuel, and more. When they came home, many of the world's fittest and best trained warriors were never the same. Headaches. Numbness. Dizziness. A cancer that would put them in a flag-draped coffin. I know. One of those soldiers was my son Major Beau Biden. We don't know for sure if a burn pit was the cause of his brain cancer, or the diseases of so many of our troops. But I'm committed to finding out everything we can."[32] (Brain cancer has occurred at unusually high rates among veterans exposed to burn pits. Medical researchers suspect a link with inhalation of titanium dust particles.[33]) A week after his speech, Biden urged Congress to pass legislation aiding veterans who'd been exposed to toxic chemicals.

During two decades, the government had subjected to administrative erasure most of the veterans who'd been exposed to toxins from burn pits. By 2022, estimates put the number of "toxic-exposed" veterans at 3.5 million.[34] "Experts are often uncertain of the direct link between specific cancers or diseases and the burn pits in Afghanistan and Iraq, where the military often burned large amounts of waste—including plastics, batteries or vehicle parts—that released plumes of dangerous chemicals into the air," the *Washington Post* reported. "Veterans then have to prove there is a direct connection between their cancer and the burn pit chemicals, a threshold that can at times be difficult to meet, particularly if the condition doesn't develop until years after a deployment. Studies have shown that Veterans Affairs rejects the vast majority of claims."[35] Finally, legislation to expand health care for veterans who'd been exposed to burn pits got through Congress and onto the Oval Office desk for Joe Biden's signature in August 2022.[36]

Biden's State of the Union speech had created momentum toward the new law, but he greatly understated the problem. What the president called "toxic smoke" has been normal not only in war zones but also in the United States. Investigative journalist Pat Elder explained that Biden omitted "most of the problem associated with open burning and open detonation of military waste." Elder, who founded the MilitaryPoisons.org website, filled in what the speech had left blank: "The military incinerates munitions, unexploded ordnance, and petroleum products in giant mushroom clouds that send toxins into the air we breathe. Chemicals, paint, medical and human waste, metals, aluminum, plastics, rubber, wood, and food waste are routinely incinerated by the Department of Defense in locations across the country." And Elder added, "The really sad thing is that President Biden only skimmed the surface on the burning of military waste. The Department of Defense regularly burns many times more waste in the U.S. than it ever did in Afghanistan or Iraq. . . . In open burning, materials such as rocket fuel are destroyed by self-sustained combustion after being ignited. In open detonation, explosives and munitions are destroyed by a detonation of added explosive charges. These practices contaminate soil, groundwater, surface water, and wildlife in surrounding communities."[37]

AFTER WRECKING AFGHANISTAN in the name of a war on terror, the U.S. government showed scant interest in helping to resuscitate or rebuild it. The intermittent talk of nation-building had revolved around enhancing the prospects that an allied government could rule. During the twenty years of the U.S. military's heavy engagement, providing material aid for the well-being of Afghan people was hardly high on Washington's to-do list.[38] But after American forces left Afghanistan in the summer of 2021, the not-so-benign neglect turned more callous, with mass starvation on the horizon as winter approached. Before the year ended, reports of dire malnutrition in the country were widespread.

The response from the U.S. government was to maintain sanctions. As *The Nation* magazine explained, "Following the Taliban takeover, the Biden administration froze $9.5 billion in Afghan assets and imposed sanctions that have devastated an already fragile economy. . . . President Joe Biden promised to promote human rights on the world stage, but his administration is now overseeing a sanctions regime that has pushed Afghanistan to the brink of famine."[39] During the fall of 2021, many humanitarian groups and activists sounded frantic alarms—first and foremost about an extreme shortage of food. The conditions were terrible and rapidly getting worse. "It is urgent that we act efficiently and effectively to speed up and scale up our delivery in Afghanistan before winter cuts off a large part of the country, with millions of people—including farmers, women, young children, and the elderly—going hungry in the freezing winter," the head of the UN's Food and Agriculture Organization said in late October 2021. He added, "We cannot wait and see humanitarian disasters unfolding in front of us—it is unacceptable."[40]

But it was acceptable to the U.S. government, which blocked and withheld desperately needed help rather than protect Afghan people from starvation. It was as if, after riding in on apocalyptic horses of war for twenty years, the United States was willing to give a wink and a nod to other horsemen of the apocalypse—famine and persistent death.

When winter arrived, so did starvation. "While Afghanistan has suffered from malnutrition for decades, the country's hunger crisis has drastically worsened in recent months," the *New York Times* reported on December 4. "This winter, an

estimated 22.8 million people—more than half the population—are expected to face potentially life-threatening levels
of food insecurity, according to an analysis by the United
Nations World Food Program and Food and Agriculture
Organization. Of those, 8.7 million people are nearing famine—the worst stage of a food crisis."

The newspaper added that "emaciated children and anemic
mothers have flooded into the malnutrition wards of hospitals, many of those facilities bereft of medical supplies that
donor aid once provided."[41] But the U.S. government, ostensibly so concerned about Afghan people for two decades,
shirked responsibility for saving those "emaciated children
and anemic mothers" and many other Afghan people facing
death that winter. The famine just wasn't a pressing concern of key U.S. policy makers. Yet they were certainly on
notice. For instance, the *Times* had printed the above-quoted
story on its front page. But a month later, the situation was
much worse. "Afghanistan Has Become the World's Largest
Humanitarian Crisis," a *New Yorker* headline blared in early
January 2022. "Four months after the Biden administration
withdrew U.S. troops, more than 20 million Afghans are on
the brink of famine."[42]

For official Washington, the starving children and all the
rest of the unfortunate Afghans were far away. Not like the
families of the senators, representatives, cabinet members,
deputy secretaries, Pentagon generals, and State Department
experts with their own precious children.

In mid-January 2022, the U.S. government announced that
it would be donating $308 million in humanitarian aid for
people in Afghanistan.[43] That could sound like a lot, but—
amounting to eight dollars per person in a country already

beset by widespread starvation in the midst of famine—it was way too little and too late. "The number of people going hungry has risen dramatically since September when the UN's World Food Program said 14 million did not have enough to eat," NBC News reported on the last day of January. "Now the world's largest humanitarian organization focused on food says that 8.7 million people are at risk of starvation. . . . The lack of funding has battered Afghanistan's already troubled economy—international support for Afghanistan was suspended and billions of dollars of the country's assets abroad, mostly in the United States, were frozen after the Taliban takeover."[44]

For many months, activists and humanitarian aid groups had been imploring President Biden to end the U.S. freeze on Afghanistan's foreign reserves. Days before Christmas in 2021, forty-eight Democrats in the House of Representatives sent an urgent letter to Biden. Emphasizing that "millions of Afghans could run out of food before winter, with 1 million children at risk of starvation," the letter pleaded for immediate action. It stressed the need to return the frozen assets to Afghanistan's central bank: "By denying international reserves to Afghanistan's private sector—including more than $7 billion belonging to Afghanistan and deposited at the Federal Reserve—the U.S. government is impacting the general population. We fear, as aid groups do, that maintaining this policy could cause more civilian deaths in the coming year than were lost in twenty years of war."[45]

On February 11, 2022—nearly eight weeks after Biden received that congressional letter—news broke about his response.[46] The president issued an executive order that split $7 billion of frozen Afghan assets between an Afghanistan relief trust fund and relatives of 9/11 victims.[47] Biden asserted emergency powers to control the money, which had belonged to Afghanistan's government when it fell in August 2021. The order siphoned off 50 percent of the funds that could have bolstered aid for Afghan people. Astute observers recognized Biden's move as domestic political pandering that would, in effect, extend the U.S. government's record of killing innocent Afghans long after the last of American forces had withdrawn. "I cannot describe for you in words how outrageous this is," commentator Mehdi Hasan tweeted. "Afghans are starving, this is all *their* money, & there was not a single Afghan aboard any of those 4 planes on 9/11."[48]

With acts of omission and commission, war was continuing by other means. For twenty years, Afghans had suffered from the U.S. military's pursuit of the Taliban—and after withdrawal of U.S. troops, Afghan civilians were still suffering and dying as the American efforts shifted to imposing draconian sanctions and diverting billions of dollars in assets. If, as Carl von Clausewitz theorized, "war is the continuation of politics by other means," U.S. policies indicated that the reverse was also true.

In pursuit of its aims, the U.S. government was continuing to treat as disposable those who happened to be living in the wrong country at the wrong time. In 2022, badly malnourished and starving Afghan civilians were no more worthy of consideration than wounded or dead Afghan civilians had been in 2012 or 2002. Scrape away the veneering platitudes of public relations, and cold hard steel remains intact. President Biden's maneuver to divert $3.5 billion of Afghan money from Afghanistan exuded a deathly smell.

While almost all of the U.S. mainline media and political establishment took it in stride, some independent outlets and experts were apoplectic. An article from *The Intercept* appeared under the headline "Biden's Decision on Frozen Afghanistan Money Is Tantamount to Mass Murder." A reader who might think the headline alarmist was left to ponder this sentence below it: "A senior Democratic foreign policy aide, who was granted anonymity to openly share his thoughts on the Biden administration's actions, said the policy 'effectively amounts to mass murder.'"[49] The destructive effects were underscored by economist Mark Weisbrot, co-director of the Center for Economic and Policy Research, who said: "If a country doesn't have reserves, and it doesn't have a functioning central bank, then there's no amount of aid that's going to come anywhere close to making up for that."[50]

Senators willing to speak out for saving uncountable Afghan lives were scarce. Weeks before Biden's decision, Bernie Sanders had been clear, saying "I urge the Biden administration to immediately release billions in frozen Afghan government funds to help avert this crisis, and prevent the death of millions of people."[51] Senator Chris Murphy, often a waffler on key foreign policy matters, said: "I believe that it's time for us to release the money."[52] Sanders and Murphy were exceptions to the prevailing indifference. "Other senators have mostly dismissed questions about America's complicity in a potential Afghan genocide," *The Intercept* reported, with Republicans and Democrats routinely unwilling to lift a senatorial tongue to advocate for saving the lives of people in a country that had been subjected to U.S. warfare for so long. When the matter of sanctions and the frozen assets was broached in a question to a Democratic senator from Hawaii,

Mazie Hirono, she replied: "We're still talking about Afghanistan?"[53]

Such dismissive attitudes at the Capitol matched up with mainstream media sensibilities. The story of an Oval Office decision that would predictably take so many Afghan lives just didn't rate. Four days after Biden's announcement, there had been "a total of ten mentions on ABC, CBS, NBC, CNN, Fox, and MSNBC: six the day of the announcement, four the next day, and none by the third day," media critic Julie Hollar reported. "The broadcast network news shows, which have more viewers than cable news, aired exactly zero reports on the issue. CNN made seven mentions, MSNBC two and Fox one. Six of the ten were brief mentions that noted no criticism of the move."[54]

It was yet another historic, tragic moment of pivotal hypocrisy and missed opportunity that enabled the United States to kill without seeing or acknowledging the human results. "Biden's announcement offered a perfect hook for reporting on the humanitarian crisis in Afghanistan, and anyone who truly cares about the Afghan people and their rights should be tearing their hair out and screaming at the top of their lungs about this audacious injustice that will surely result in more deaths and hardship," Hollar wrote. "But despite their wailing about the Taliban's impact on Afghan women's futures, few in U.S. TV news seem concerned about those same women facing starvation as a result of U.S. policy."[55]

Extreme food scarcity during the 2021–22 winter took untold Afghan lives, while the U.S. government basically went AWOL from an international effort that rushed to limit the toll. "Humanitarian assistance helped avert a food security catastrophe over the harsh winter in Afghanistan," the United

Nations reported in midspring, but "hunger still persists at unprecedented levels." The outlook remained grim: "Nearly 20 million people in Afghanistan—almost half the population—are facing acute hunger."[56]

Marking the one-year anniversary of the American pullout, some U.S. news outlets revisited Afghanistan with sizable amounts of coverage in the late summer of 2022. Typically, there was little or no mention of severe hunger and starvation among Afghan people, while the media narratives did not shed light on culpable U.S. policies. When NPR's *Morning Edition* and *All Things Considered* devoted 114 minutes of airtime to Afghanistan during two weeks in August, the reporting included no more than forty seconds about the grave food scarcity or the dire effects of the U.S. government's refusal to return several billion dollars of Afghanistan's money.[57]

What can we conclude from this life-and-death episode that made such little impact on American public discourse and made such terrible impacts on Afghan people? Whatever the unique aspects involved, the underlying convergence of media, politics, and powerful priorities is awfully familiar. The warfare state of the United States maintains its grip at home while militarism is euphemized, accepted, internalized, and honored with silence if not praise. Habits of abstraction, buffering and blocking human connection, enable continual war and scarcely glimpsed consequences for people who are unseen and unacknowledged. Lethal cruelty dresses up as pragmatic sophistication.

Remorse not included, the war machine spins on.

CHAPTER SIX

LIVES THAT REALLY MATTER, LIVES THAT DON'T

WITH AN EXPLANATION THAT IT "SEEMS PERVERSE TO FOCUS too much on the casualties or hardship in Afghanistan," CNN's chairman Walter Isaacson issued a memo ordering the network's journalists not to portray the sometimes-fatal ordeals of Afghan civilians without emphasizing a connection to 9/11.[1] "You want to make sure people understand that when they see civilian suffering there, it's in the context of a terrorist attack that caused enormous suffering in the United States," Isaacson told a reporter three weeks after the U.S. attack on Afghanistan began.[2] Another memo in late October 2001, from the network's head of standards and practices, spelled out that compliance was mandatory: "Even though it may start sounding rote, it is important that we make this point each time."[3]

So, when correspondent Nic Robertson mentioned "several people who told us that various friends and relatives had died in the bombing there in that collateral damage," CNN anchor Judy Woodruff was quick on the uptake—as required by CNN management—immediately telling viewers: "And we would just remind you, as we always do now with these reports from inside the Taliban-controlled Afghanistan, that you're seeing only one side of the story, that these U.S. military actions that Nic Robertson was talking about are in response to a terrorist attack that killed 5,000 and more innocent people inside the United States."[4] (The verified number of 9/11 deaths was later set at 2,996.)

A nation that had been victimized by such enormous evil on 9/11 could not begin to do anything comparable. Absolution would be preemptive, echoing a character in the short story "Editha" by William Dean Howells a century earlier: "What a thing it is to have a country that *can't* be wrong, but if it is, is right, anyway!"[5]

"AL QAEDA AND THE VIOLENT extremists who you're fighting against want to destroy, but all of you want to build," President Obama told American troops in Afghanistan during a visit in the early spring of 2010, delineating the black-and-white distinction between terrorists and U.S. forces. "And that is something essential about America. They've got no respect for human life. You see dignity in every human being. That's part of what we value as Americans."[6] Truth existed in what Obama was saying. Yet there was also much untruth that conceptually vaporized the victims of U.S. warfare. As for the actual losses and grief of those on the American side, presidents see a need to tread lightly.

From the vantage point of authorities eager to encourage support for ongoing warfare, stories in need of telling pay tribute to Americans who've been killed in combat—but without giving too much public visibility to the deaths and the deep sorrow of loved ones left behind. War supporters sometimes differ on how to strike a balance.

For officeholders in Washington and laptop warriors in the press corps, over time, enthusiasm for ongoing U.S. wars generally seems inversely proportional to the number of American casualties. Flag-draped coffins arriving on conveyor belts at military bases in the United States have been bad optics. "On the eve of the Iraq invasion" in early 2003, the *Washington Post* reported, the Pentagon ordered bases to adopt a policy of "making the arrival ceremonies off limits." Tightening enforcement of restrictions that had been issued a dozen years earlier, at the time of the Gulf War, the George W. Bush administration "ended the public dissemination of such images by banning news coverage and photography of dead soldiers' homecomings on all military bases."[7] The ban stayed in effect until 2009, when it was removed by the incoming Obama administration.[8]

Those who clamored for the public to be able to see such pictures were inclined to focus on the public need to honor the American fallen. "This decision restores to its rightful, honorable place the immense value of the sacrifice American troops make on behalf of their nation," said one commentator. Another contended that the original ban on media coverage "was clearly meant to hide the cost of war."[9] But foreign civilians who died in the same wars, never to be in a red-white-and-blue casket, were implicitly reduced to the standing of nonpersons.

TEN YEARS AFTER THE INVASION of Iraq, President Obama was a couple of months into his second term, and the Iraq War was still raging. At that point, the Center for American Progress (closely aligned with the entrenched wing of the

Democratic Party) came out with what it headlined as "The Iraq War Ledger: A Look at the War's Human, Financial, and Strategic Costs." The gist was that the invasion and war had turned out to be a bad investment, gauged by criteria at the top: "This anniversary is an appropriate time to examine, once again, the costs and benefits to U.S. national security from our intervention there."[10]

The cost-benefit analysis lowballed the war's total deaths at scarcely more than one hundred thousand, while providing a disclaimer: "We would like to acknowledge that other studies, such as those carried out by the Johns Hopkins Bloomberg School of Public Health and the Iraq Family Health Survey, estimate much higher civilian deaths as a result of the war." The center's report put the casualties of U.S. forces at 4,484 dead and 32,200 wounded. In financial terms, the "Cost of Operation Iraqi Freedom" was listed at $806 billion, while the "projected total cost of veterans' health care and disability" was pegged at somewhere between $422 billion and $717 billion.

Immediately below that statistical ledger came this stand-alone statement without any elaboration: "The foregoing costs could conceivably be justified if the Iraq intervention had improved the United States' strategic position in the Middle East. But this is clearly not the case. The Iraq war has strengthened anti-U.S. elements and made the position of the United States and its allies more precarious."[11] Those three sentences, particularly the first, deserve a freeze-frame and some mulling over. The deaths, the suffering, the financial drain could conceivably be justified "if the Iraq intervention had improved the United States' strategic position in the Middle East." But alas, that was not the case. The war had been a flop.

✧

MORE THAN A QUARTER CENTURY after sending several hundred thousand U.S. troops into the 1991 Gulf War, former President George H.W. Bush tweeted: "Very much regret missing the Memorial Day parade today in Kennebunkport, and am forever grateful not only to those patriots who made the ultimate sacrifice for our Nation—but also the Gold Star families whose heritage is imbued with their honor and heroism."[12] Among those who would never be mentioned by a current or former president in connection with honor or heroism were others directly affected by the six-week Gulf War: the dead Iraqi civilians, who, according to some estimates, numbered between one hundred thousand and two hundred thousand.[13]

"Proud veterans and families of the fallen, it is a privilege to spend this Veterans Day with you," the second President Bush said at a 2007 ceremony. Speaking of "the young men we remember today," Bush said: "The valor and selfless devotion of these men fills their families with immeasurable pride. Yet this pride cannot fill the hole in their loved ones' aching hearts, or relieve the burden of grief that will remain for a lifetime." An aspect of presidential duties is to assure one and all that sacrificed young American lives have not been squandered. As Bush put it, "In their sorrow, these families need to know, and families all across the nation of the fallen need to know that your loved ones served a cause that is good, and just, and noble. And, as their commander in chief, I make you this promise: their sacrifice will not be in vain."[14]

Commanders in chief are glad to make such facile promises. Bush was merely reading from a prepared text virtually indistinguishable from President Clinton's before him and President Obama's after. While it's traditional to briefly acknowledge that grief will always painfully remain with loved ones of "the fallen," no president has ever admitted that he chose to waste young lives. Such an admission would be unthinkable. What oratory like "their sacrifice will not be in vain" really does for the families left behind is uncertain. But certainly, presidents do not say that foreigners killed by U.S. firepower also leave behind a "hole in their loved ones' aching hearts," with "the burden of grief that will remain for a lifetime." Nor do members of Congress or news media demand any such acknowledgment.

THE WAR MACHINERY DEPENDS on a steady supply of humans. For warfare, young males are the essential product.

A former Marine sniper, *Jarhead* author Anthony Swofford, told me that young men often watched pornography to psyche themselves up before going into battle during the Gulf War. When I asked about the mashed-up word "warnography," he didn't hesitate to reply that it was a very apt term; the same held true for "wargasm." The exploitation of people coming of age to go out and kill while risking their lives is an old story made new with each passing occurrence; in retrospect if not at the time, it's possible to see through the manipulation ("let's you and them fight") to glimpse the blends of cynicism and possible sincerity involved, as government officials sign the orders to keep the military's human supply chain rolling. There has been no lack of willingness if not eagerness to sacrifice the young on behalf of personal, political, and international agendas that—for the general public—remain somewhere between opaque and hidden. What the eulogizers call "the ultimate sacrifice" is not theirs.

Every decade in our lifetimes, millions of American men have passed through instruction on how to be comfortable with carrying and shooting firearms, their impulses trained on the potential to kill—explicitly encouraged at boot camp, forbidden after military discharge—as though the muscle memory and the deeply promoted synapses of emotional reflexes could be turned on and off at authority's will. Killing others has been idealized while condemned in domestic contexts. Messaging comes from news and entertainment media, the broad political establishment, and mass culture, shaping and reflecting the acceptance if not glorification of lethal violence under the color of authority. Folded flags and star-spangled caskets are made visible for brief periods of time; the mourners and their mourning soon fade into public invisibility. Those who will never return are heroes in mortal absentia, unable to be present to affirm or dispute the nobility of their involvement in warfare. Anyone they might have killed would be mourned by a different set of loved ones, unseen through the usual American lens as mere cyphers—mystified nothings.

FORMER U.S. ARMY intelligence analyst Chelsea Manning spent seven years in a military prison—including long, torturous stretches in solitary confinement—for making possible the public disclosure of such evidence as the instantly infamous "Collateral Murder" video that showed the cavalier killing of eleven Iraqi civilians from the air.[15] After bringing that video into the open and also releasing huge troves of documents that exposed deceptions, cover-ups, and massacres of civilians by the U.S. military, WikiLeaks publisher Julian Assange underwent seven years of asylum in Ecuador's small London embassy and then went to prison, with scant prospects for release before reaching old age. As the U.S. government labored to gather evidence against Assange for publishing official secrets, Manning refused to testify—and, in 2019, ended up back in prison for two more stints behind bars. The first stretch lasted two months, which included twenty-eight days in solitary confinement. Released when the initial grand jury expired, she was soon back in prison yet again after refusing to give testimony to the new one. By the end of 2019, she had spent more than three-quarters of the year in prison, often under conditions that a UN investigator publicly likened to torture.[16]

How to explain why someone who endured so many years in prison under conditions that had driven her to deep despair and attempting suicide would, after twenty-two months on the outside, willingly return to such conditions rather than testify to a grand jury? Manning spoke of why she was standing her ground. "I believe this grand jury seeks to undermine the integrity of public discourse with the aim of punishing those who expose any serious, ongoing, and systemic abuses of power by this government, as well as the rest of the international community," she said. Awful as imprisonment was for her, Manning made clear that betraying her conscience by aiding the persecution of Assange for publishing truth about wars would be even worse: "Over the past decade, I grappled with bouts of depression. I can think of nothing that could exacerbate those struggles more than pretending to live as someone I am not once again, and turning my back on everything I care about and fight for."[17]

When a judge finally gave up and released Manning for good in mid-March 2020, she had been in prison another fifty-two weeks simply for refusing to rat on Assange in front of a grand jury. Wording in the judge's order was revealing: "The court finds Ms. Manning's appearance before the grand jury is no longer needed, in light of which her detention no longer serves any coercive purpose." After all, coercion was a key purpose, to bend Manning to the government's will (while discouraging would-be emulators). In this case, the judge was conceding that coercion had failed. Yet the federal court system was not done with its antiwar prisoner of conscience. As a follow-up penalty for her recalcitrance, the same judicial order that freed Manning also levied a fine of $256,000, "due and payable immediately to the clerk."[18]

A system of silence found Manning's active noncooperation to be intolerable. But why? The objectification and erasure of certain war victims are essential for the warfare state.

Chelsea Manning was one of the precious few whistleblowers who had the clarity of mind and heart to share vital information with the public, not just disclosing "mistakes" but also bringing to light patterns of war crimes and—by clear implication—the stateside complicity of supposed innocence, part genuine cluelessness, part disingenuous fakery.

WEEKS AFTER PRESIDENT BIDEN took office, Inter Press Service described the continuing horrors in Yemen:

The United Nations has rightly described the deaths and devastation in war-ravaged Yemen as the "world's worst humanitarian disaster"—caused mostly by widespread air attacks on civilians by a coalition led [by] Saudi Arabia and the United Arab Emirates. But rarely, if ever, has the world denounced the primary arms merchants, including the U.S. and U.K., for the more than 100,000 killings since 2015—despite accusations of "war crimes" by human rights organizations. The killings are due mostly to air strikes on weddings, funerals, private homes, villages, and schools. Additionally, over 130,000 have died resulting largely from war-related shortages of food and medical care. . . . And despite concerns in the U.S. and U.K. about Saudi Arabia's military intervention in Yemen, both weapons suppliers continued to export arms to Saudi Arabia—with 73 percent of Saudi Arabia's arms imports originating in the U.S. and 13 percent from the U.K.[19]

After entering the White House, Biden did not follow through on campaign vows to curtail U.S. support for the Saudi war. Instead, his administration approved billions of dollars in weapons sales to Saudi Arabia and the United Arab Emirates, while continuing to provide logistical support, maintenance, and spare parts to the Royal Saudi Air Force. The catastrophe continued without letup.

"Yemen remains one of the largest humanitarian crises in the world, with around 21 million people in need of humanitarian assistance, including more than 11 million children," UNICEF reported in early 2022. "Since the conflict escalated in March 2015, the country has become a living hell for the country's children. . . . Yemen has been plagued by one of the world's worst food crises, with nearly 2.3 million children under the age of five suffering from acute malnutrition. Of these, 400,000 are expected to suffer from severe acute malnutrition and could die if they do not receive urgent treatment."[20]

The United States and its British junior partner "have participated in the war by providing intelligence to help the Saudi-led coalition conduct bombing raids . . . and supplying crucial parts for war planes that are necessary to continue bombing raids, among other support," the DC-based organization Just Foreign Policy said after more than a year of the Biden administration. "The U.S. has continued to do this despite clear evidence of mass civilian casualties and purposeful starvation of the Yemini populace that many experts say amounts to genocide."[21]

When President Biden visited Saudi Arabia in mid-July 2022, the lasting image was his fist bump with crown prince Mohammed bin Salman, the kingdom's de facto ruler. It was "a picture that will define this visit—everything the Saudis could have hoped for," the BBC noted.[22] American media widely reported the president's assertion that he had raised with the prince his direct role[23] in the 2018 murder of journalist Jamal Khashoggi—a killing that had been the subject of immense publicity for years—but news coverage hardly mentioned bin Salman's direct role in the war that took hundreds of thousands of Yemeni lives. An unspoken takeaway was that the deaths and suffering in Yemen counted for little.

To U.S. news outlets, overall, the ongoing disaster in Yemen was no big deal. Notwithstanding the pivotal role of the U.S. government, the suffering and the deaths didn't add up to drawing more than intermittent and fragmented media attention, if any. The pattern was long-standing.

At the end of 2017, after nearly three years of the war in Yemen, the media watchdog group Fairness and Accuracy In Reporting (FAIR) did an in-depth study examining MSNBC's news coverage of the humanitarian crisis. The research discovered that there had been virtually no coverage at all: "An analysis by FAIR has found that the leading liberal cable network did not run a single segment devoted specifically to Yemen in the second half of 2017. . . . Moreover, in all of 2017, MSNBC only aired one broadcast on the U.S.-backed Saudi airstrikes that have killed thousands of Yemeni civilians. And it never mentioned the impoverished nation's colossal cholera epidemic, which infected more than 1 million Yemenis in the largest outbreak in recorded history." The study noted that media coverage was absent while the U.S. government played a leading role in the war on Yemen, "selling many billions of dollars of weapons to Saudi Arabia, refueling Saudi warplanes as they relentlessly bomb civilian areas, and providing intelligence and military assistance to the Saudi air force."[24]

While MSNBC was so scrupulously avoiding coverage of the continual calamities in Yemen during the Trump presidency, the network was fixated on Russia. "MSNBC ran nearly 5,000 percent more segments that mentioned Russia than segments that mentioned Yemen," the FAIR research showed. In the process, the news channel's programmers banished to airtime oblivion the people in Yemen who were dying from bombs, malnutrition, and cholera. The network ignored the horrendous magnitude of the human suffering as well as the U.S. government's role in perpetuating it.

But the ratings and fame climbed for MSNBC and its star anchors, especially Rachel Maddow,[25] who devoted hundreds of prime-time hours to "Russiagate." Meanwhile, they ignored the increasing danger that tensions between Washington and Moscow might escalate into an omnicidal war between the world's two nuclear superpowers.[26]

And if that happens, the victims of war will have the ultimate invisibility.

BY THE TIME President Biden gave his State of the Union address in early March 2022, days after Russia invaded Ukraine, the dangers of nuclear war were the gravest since the Cuban Missile Crisis sixty years earlier.[27] Cold War winds were approaching gale force. Russian president Vladimir Putin had just ordered his country's nuclear arsenal to go on heightened alert. The United States and allies were stepping up arms shipments to Ukrainian forces. The escalation was spiraling. Yet not one of Biden's 6,500 words mentioned nuclear weapons or the darkening shadow of potential apocalypse that hung over the world. Nor did the president's speech go anywhere near acknowledging that risks of nuclear war—as symbolized by the creeping hands of the "Doomsday Clock" maintained by the *Bulletin of the Atomic Scientists*—had steadily moved upward during the last decade, reaching one hundred seconds to midnight in 2022 compared to six minutes to midnight a dozen years earlier.[28]

Official silences might seem to dispel frightening realities, making them no more visible than gaslight in mist. But, for more than seventy-five years, the specter of nuclear annihilation had never really stopped haunting. And no matter what officials said as war escalated in Ukraine during 2022, what they didn't say—and what they implicitly prompted us not to see—loomed in the stark light provided by Albert Einstein in January 1947, when he wrote about the release of atomic energy: "This basic power of the universe cannot be fitted into the outmoded concept of narrow nationalisms. For there is no secret and there is no defense, there is no possibility of control except through the aroused understanding and insistence of the peoples of the world." Einstein expressed a belief that "an informed citizenry will act for life and not death."[29] But shrouding nuclear realities in haze has encouraged citizenry to be uninformed and inactive.

Few journalists with major media outlets have wandered far enough away from the conventional ruts along Pennsylvania Avenue to illuminate how much the U.S. government has done to undermine significant nuclear arms control. In 2002, the George W. Bush administration withdrew from the Anti-Ballistic Missile Treaty, a vital pact that had been in effect for thirty years; negotiated during the Nixon administration, the treaty between Washington and Moscow declared that its limits would be a "substantial factor in curbing the race in strategic offensive arms."[30] Despite his promising rhetoric, President Obama plunged ahead to begin a $1.7 trillion program for further developing U.S. nuclear forces under the euphemism of "modernization." President Trump pulled the United States out of the Intermediate-Range Nuclear Forces Treaty, which had eliminated an entire category of missiles from Europe since the late 1980s. By killing the ABM[31] and INF[32] agreements, the United States pushed the world farther away from control of nuclear weaponry.

Tensions worsened with the expansion of NATO to Russia's borders, as the United States ignored the vehement Russian opposition to enlarging the military alliance. Also ignored was an unequivocal warning from the establishment's foreign policy sage George F. Kennan, who said in 1997 that "expanding NATO would be the most fateful error of American policy in the post–Cold War era."[33] Between 1999 and 2004, NATO expanded into ten Eastern European countries. Among them, Poland and Romania became hosts for ongoing deployment of ABM systems; while touted as "defensive," those systems could be retrofitted with offensive cruise missiles.[34]

Few Americans were informed about the significance of such developments or how it all might look when viewed through Kremlin windows. Reverence and adulation regularly gushed toward NATO from official Washington and U.S. media. About reviled societies, we hear labels like "propaganda." In the United States, assumed truisms can be laundered and flatironed as common sense.

Any "conventional" war putting Russia and the United States in direct conflict has the major potential of being a tripwire to set off a nuclear conflagration. Heightened tensions lead to paranoia and greater likelihood of mistaking a false alarm for the real thing. This is especially dangerous because of land-based intercontinental ballistic missiles (ICBMs), which are uniquely vulnerable to attack and therefore remain on hair-trigger, launch-on-warning alert. Four hundred of those missiles, fully armed and ready to fire from underground silos, are scattered across prairies and hardscrabble terrain in Colorado, Montana, Nebraska, North Dakota, and Wyoming.

While their locations are not secret, the actual implications of the ICBMs get scant notice. "These missiles are some of the most dangerous weapons in the world," former Defense secretary William Perry warned in 2016. "They could even trigger an accidental nuclear war."[35] As Daniel Ellsberg and I wrote in *The Nation* five years later, "Contrary to uninformed assumptions, discarding all ICBMs could be accomplished unilaterally by the United States with no downside. Even if Russia chose not to follow suit, dismantling the potentially cataclysmic land-based missiles would make the world safer for everyone on the planet."[36] But the dangers of ICBMs and the wisdom of eliminating them have never been more than tiny blips on the nation's screens.

AS 2022 GOT UNDERWAY, the man who had led the top-level deception for invading Iraq visited the floor of the House of Representatives. "Dick Cheney, Once a Villain to Democrats, Hailed in Surprise Capitol Visit to Mark January 6," said a *USA Today* headline.[37] "All seemed forgiven," the newspaper reported, "as young and old House Democrats came up to speak with the former vice president." There was a lot to forgive. As vice president, Cheney had been the single most important orchestrator and amplifier of falsehoods that propelled the country into the Iraq War that was to directly result in thousands of American deaths, hundreds of thousands of Iraqi deaths, and devastation of the invaded country. But in 2022, the praise for the ex-VP extended to conveying a forgive-and-forget message, as though all the killing and suffering could now be set aside in the light of history, as though the carnage and vast destruction were, in retrospect, no big deal.

The former vice president was on the House floor to support his daughter, Congresswoman Liz Cheney, one of the few elected Republicans to completely denounce President Trump's role in the assault on the Capitol a year earlier. For Democratic leaders, that was enough to roll out the blue carpet. House Speaker Nancy Pelosi shook Dick Cheney's hand and later told reporters: "We were very honored by his being there."[38] For the House Democrats' leader to so effusively welcome Cheney, to be "very honored" by his presence, was a way of saying that bygones could be bygones. One might wonder if the Congress members who lined up to shake the elder Cheney's hand would have been so warm to him if a loved one's body had been shattered by the war he lied the nation into.

The "honored" response was not only a blinkered look back. It was also a prefigurative way of saying that the same could end up being the case in relation to future wars. A leader could launch the country into war on a mendacious basis, yet sooner or later it all wouldn't necessarily amount to much in public arenas of media and politics. To some, this added up to nothing more than the political axiom of having no permanent friends or permanent enemies. To others, this signified that, in the United States, being a major war criminal was fully compatible with receiving praise from the powerful, influential, and admired.

And so it was, not only for the bottom of the Bush-Cheney presidency but also for the top. Television icon Ellen DeGeneres made a point of publicly socializing with former president George W. Bush—accompanying him to a football game in October 2019 and then sharing video of him sitting next to her in the stands. DeGeneres showed the video on her TV program and read aloud a tweet she received that said "Ellen and George Bush together makes me have faith in America again."[39] DeGeneres then told the audience (which responded with thunderous applause): "I'm friends with George Bush. In fact, I'm friends with a lot of people who don't share the same beliefs that I have. . . . But just because I don't agree with someone on everything doesn't mean that I'm not going to be friends with them. When I say, 'be kind to one another,' I don't only mean only the people that think the same way that you do. I mean be kind to everyone—doesn't matter."[40]

At first glance, that might seem like a testimonial to civility. Or to incongruity. "Be kind to everyone" is consistent with befriending a former president who used deception to start a war that took countless lives?

For Michelle Obama, the answer was also yes. The same man who had sat in the Oval Office and proclaimed himself to be "the decider" for U.S. warfare based on lies was, a few years later, just plain lovable. As with Pelosi and DeGeneres, the forgiveness was not the former first lady's to give, but she was evidently pleased to give it anyway. In December 2019, Michelle Obama explained her friendship with Bush on national television. "Our values are the same," she said. "We disagree on policy but we don't disagree on humanity. We don't disagree about love and compassion."[41]

It was a way of conveying that the war dead did not really matter much, after all.

CHAPTER SEVEN

THE COLOR
OF WAR

THE ACCLAIMED HUMAN RIGHTS ADVOCATE HASSAN
El-Tayyab knew his way around Capitol Hill, where he had
pulled together numerous meetings with congressional staffers and members of key committees. He'd also broken new
ground while informing journalists about a wide range of
immense suffering in war zones. By the time Russia invaded
Ukraine in late February 2022, El-Tayyab—based at the
Friends Committee on National Legislation—was an old
hand at working to generate compassion and help for victims of wars. The new war set off a tremendous amount of
empathetic media coverage that focused on the anguish and
deaths of Ukraine's war victims, in sharp contrast to the
meager amounts of such coverage by the same media outlets
about countries where the war victims were casualties of the
United States' armed forces or allies. After a week of American media's wall-to-wall spotlight on Ukraine war horrors,
El-Tayyab accused U.S. news outlets of "blatantly display-
ing racism by only adequately covering a war between white
people. In comparison, we see almost no coverage of wars in
Yemen, Afghanistan, Syria, Palestine, Somalia, Ethiopia, etc.
Implication is white lives matter more to them than black/
brown lives."[1]

The tenor and volume of U.S. media coverage have routinely hinged on who is doing the killing and who is being killed. When American armed forces are inflicting the carnage, the chances of deeply sympathetic coverage of the killed, wounded, and bereaved are greatly diminished—but when the killers are adversaries of the U.S. government, the media floodgates of compassion and human connection open wide. Such selective empathy was on overwhelming display as Ukraine withstood the barbaric Russian assault. The newsletter of Fairness and Accuracy In Reporting printed a sardonic headline: "Turns Out Corporate Media Can Oppose War—When an Official Enemy Is the Aggressor."[2]

"The Ukrainian people are presented as brave frontline fighters from all walks of life, inspired to pick up arms in defense of their land," journalist Eoin Higgins observed. At the same time, "the way the media has been describing their fight and the conflict is telling audiences more than just the story of the people of Ukraine's fight against invasion. The coverage betrays deep-seated bias in whose struggles against oppression are considered worthy and whose are not; and, in some cases, showing just how insidious the ideas of 'us and them' and 'civilization' really are."[3]

Key elements of such media bias include hypernationalism and racial prejudice, apt to coagulate into cultural chauvinism. Reporting from Ukraine's capital, Kyiv, CBS News television correspondent Charlie D'Agata told viewers: "This isn't a place, with all due respect, like Iraq or Afghanistan, that has seen conflict raging for decades. This is a relatively civilized, relatively European—I have to choose those words carefully, too—city, where you wouldn't expect that or hope that it's going to happen."[4] D'Agata later apologized. But such statements were merely tips of customary icebergs.

Soon after the Ukraine invasion began, the Arab and Middle Eastern Journalists Association issued an already badly needed statement urging all news organizations "to be mindful of implicit and explicit bias in their coverage of war in Ukraine." The organization added, "In only the last few days, we have tracked examples of racist news coverage that ascribes more importance to some victims of war over others. . . . This type of commentary reflects the pervasive mentality in Western journalism of normalizing tragedy in parts of the world such as the Middle East, Africa, South Asia, and Latin America. It dehumanizes and renders their experience with war as somehow normal and expected." That kind of media coverage "contributes to the erasure of populations around the world who continue to experience violent occupation and aggression."[5]

Such erasure—journalistic, psychological, political—has always been a "war on terror" subtext. By contrast, it surfaced into plain view with the sudden and continuing explosion of U.S. media empathy for war victims in Ukraine. The goal of critiques was not at all to begrudge the hugely sympathetic news coverage of Ukraine's war victims. The essential point was that a single standard of humanity should infuse media coverage of wars, everywhere and always.

"Journalists reporting on Russia's invasion of Ukraine could not help but compare the military strikes and resulting humanitarian crisis to recent conflicts in the Middle East and Afghanistan," *Los Angeles Times* television critic Lorraine Ali wrote five days after the invasion began. "But a painful double standard quickly emerged inside of those comparisons." She added:

In the heat of war, as the international press corps scrambled in real time to wrap their arms around a fast-moving military campaign, a number of correspondents, consciously or not, framed suffering and displacement as acceptable for Arabs, Afghans and others *over there*— but not here, in Europe, where the people "have blue eyes and blond hair" and where they "look like us." (And yes, those are actual quotations from news clips.) The sentiment has been laid bare again and again in numerous American and European press outlets since the beginning of the invasion last week. . . . Writers who'd previously addressed conflicts in the Gulf region, often with a focus on geopolitical strategy and employing moral abstractions, appeared to be empathizing for the first time with the plight of civilians.[6]

The heavily publicized flight of Ukrainians from their suddenly war-torn country was a catalyst for reporter Nick Turse's vivid memories of witnessing the ordeals of refugees in Africa. "In 2018, I watched as a postage-stamp-sized camp for displaced people in Ituri Province in the far east of the Democratic Republic of Congo mushroomed from hundreds of people to more than 10,000, spilling beyond its borders and necessitating the creation of another sprawling encampment across town," he wrote. Congo's refugee crisis was ongoing. "Around 2.7 million Congolese were driven from their homes between January and November 2021, according to the United Nations, swelling the grand total of internally displaced people in that country to 5.6 million."[7]

Turse recounted a trip to the small West African country of Burkina Faso in 2020, when he "watched an unfolding humanitarian catastrophe. Families were streaming down that road from Barsalogho about 100 miles north of the capital, Ouagadougou, toward Kaya, a market town whose population had almost doubled that year. They were victims of a war without a name, a lethal contest between Islamist terrorists who massacre without compunction and government forces that have killed more civilians than militants."

With 84 million people in the world "forcibly displaced by war, persecution, general violence, or human-rights violations" in 2021 alone, Turse concluded, "The very least the world's comfortable classes could do is throw money at the problem. The U.S. government—responsible for up to 60 million displaced people in Afghanistan, Iraq, Libya, Pakistan, the Philippines, Somalia, Syria, and Yemen due to its war on terror—bears a special responsibility, but hasn't stepped up." We live on a globe wracked by wars and related disruptions causing vast misery, overwhelmingly for people of color, a perennial emergency that is scantily covered by the media of the wealthiest nation. "Our arbitrary borders, miserly aid, and cruel policies," Turse wrote, "ensure that those most victimized by conflict will remain adrift, wandering the planet in search of safety, discarded by the rest of us as marginal people on the margins of an unforgiving world."[8]

AS RUSSIA'S WAR ON UKRAINE continued, journalist Peter Beinart raised an astute question: "When discussing domestic policy, progressive commentators often note that American police respond more harshly to Black protesters than white ones and that the media describes opioid-addicted rural white Americans as victims but drug-addicted urban Black Americans as depraved. Why wouldn't these racial disparities shape American foreign policy too?"[9]

Racial prejudice combines with support for the gist of U.S. foreign policy to slant media coverage of wars and international relations. As a matter of course, mainstream journalists and news organizations are risk averse—disinclined to challenge Washington's claims about who is (so to speak) wearing black hats and white hats in clashes overseas. Hypocrisies and double standards go unnoticed or at least unmentioned. Irony-free zones abound.

James Zogby, president of the Arab American Institute, was on target when he pointed out, "It passed without comment in the U.S. press when an Israeli government official denounced the Russian invasion as a 'grave violation of the international order,' while another expressed his government's support for Ukraine's 'territorial integrity and sovereignty'—as if Israel has ever respected these concepts. They have invaded and occupied Lebanon, Syria, Palestine, and Egypt, justifying their actions using the same 'security' argument claimed by the Russians."[10] Meanwhile, Senator Bernie Sanders's foreign policy adviser Matt Duss had this to say: "As a Ukrainian-American I am immensely proud of the bravery of Ukrainians and of the support being shown by Americans. As a Middle East analyst I am floored by the blatant double standard on resisting occupation and repression."[11]

Noting that Israel has been imposing "violent occupation for more than fifty years," columnist Gideon Levy wrote in the Israeli daily newspaper *Haaretz* that "Russia's justification for an invasion, the propaganda and the lies, seem taken from Israel's playbook every time it invaded Gaza or Lebanon. Israel always feels threatened, just like Russia, and both deny the national rights of the people it occupies." Levy asked, "Why does the Israeli heart go out to the Ukrainian refugees and the victims of horror and fear there, but is indifferent to the suffering and the fear in Gaza and the expulsion of Palestinians who are refugees?"[12] The Israeli indifference has mirrored American indifference toward victims of war and occupation who are assumed to be unworthy of front-and-center visibility, let alone compassion or support.

As a U.S. ally, Israel eludes much critical scrutiny in American media, notwithstanding its occupation of Gaza and the West Bank, repeatedly deemed illegal by the UN Security Council.[13] Leading human rights organizations—including Amnesty International, Human Rights Watch, and Israel's B'Tselem—have described Israeli policies toward Palestinians as "apartheid."[14] And Washington is anything but a mere bystander. By 2022, Israel and the United States were midway through an unprecedented ten-year pact that committed at least $38 billion in military aid from the U.S. government.[15] Israel's white English-speaking leaders and spokespeople have long been adept at spinning their way past systematically inhuman treatment of Palestinian people. Palestinians—Arabic-speaking and predominantly Muslim—are easily, whether or not consciously, cast as "others." Their suffering under military occupation—sometimes escalating into lethal violence, with Palestinians of all ages dying far more often than Israelis—is rarely visible to American news consumers.

And so, when U.S. media lavished adulation on Ukrainians for resisting Russian troops that had invaded to occupy their homeland, the ironies jumped out at Zogby:

Early in the invasion, there were two short film clips that went viral on various social media platforms. One showed a little child playing and then being incinerated by an aerial bombardment. The other featured a little girl hitting a soldier, twice her size, shouting at him that he should go back to his country. Both the child victim and the girl were presented as Ukrainians, while the killer bomb and the soldier were claimed to be Russian. Neither was the case. The first was a Palestinian killed in an Israeli air assault in Gaza, and the second was a Palestinian girl, Ahed Tamimi, who was later arrested for striking an Israeli soldier. In the same vein, on the day that American TV outlets were showing "heroic" Ukrainians stockpiling Molotov cocktails for use against the Russian invaders, a fourteen-year-old Palestinian boy was shot dead for throwing a Molotov cocktail at an Israeli settler's car. The obvious point was that it's not what you do, but who you are that determines how you are to be seen.[16]

Or, in news media, if you will be seen at all.

CERTAIN WORDS THAT ENTERED the American lexicon in the process of making war—vile, dehumanizing words such as "gooks" (Vietnam) and "ragheads" (the Middle East)—tell us nothing about the people being vilified but much about the people doing the vilifying. You could call it ethical depravity or spiritual illness, or use more traditional terms like prejudice or bigotry—but whatever the labels, the history of U.S.

wars in Asia, the Middle East, Africa, and Latin America has exuded a stench of white supremacy, discounting the value of lives at the other end of U.S. bullets, bombs, and missiles.

Yet racial factors in war-making decisions get very little mention in U.S. media and virtually none in the political world of officials in Washington. The pretense is that racism had nothing to do with decisions for warfare in Vietnam, Laos, Cambodia, Grenada, Panama, Iraq, Afghanistan, Libya, and elsewhere. Of course, the Pentagon's bombs didn't fall on those countries just because they were inhabited by people of color—but the fact that they were inhabited by people of color made it easier to start and continue waging war in their countries. To contend otherwise would be to claim that racism does not hold significant sway over public attitudes, political institutions, and the overall power structure of the United States: a claim that would be widely dismissed as noncredible in domestic contexts of a nation that remains rife with institutional racism, from police and courts, to state legislatures and Congress, to financial systems and economic structures.

"Race is not a perspective on international relations; it is a central organizing feature of world politics," scholars Kelebogile Zvobgo and Meredith Loken wrote in 2020. Observing that "today race shapes threat perception and responses to violent extremism, inside and outside the 'war on terror,'" they contended that "one cannot comprehend world politics while ignoring race and racism. . . . Race continues to shape international and domestic threat perceptions and consequent foreign policy; international responses to immigrants and refugees; and access to health and environmental stability."[17]

Skewed views of warfare's victims are facilitated by layers of personal and collective racism, conscious or not, that we know or should know persist in the United States. To pretend otherwise—which mass media and the politically powerful do—is to engage in a silent form of gaslighting that sets aside people whose voices are not heard, whose faces are not seen, whose names or lives are not known, all of which makes the killing and the ignoring easier. Those who suffer from U.S. military actions overseas are relegated to a kind of psychological apartheid; separate and unequal, not of much importance.

The rhetoric of the "war on terror" supplied a smokescreen that made it harder to see how militarism and racism were fondling each other in a death grip. Hidden in plain sight was the reality that just about every targeted or untargeted victim of U.S. warfare in the twenty-first century was a person of color.

"The intertwined histories of race and empire haunt the present," in the words of Duncan Bell, a professor of political thought and international relations at the University of Cambridge.[18] Also writing in 2020, Oxford scholar Nima Gerami called for "an open and honest debate about the ways race and racism have influenced America's foreign policy for centuries, perpetuating racial injustice and inequality abroad in the name of national security."

Gerami wasn't satisfied with the ascension of such figures as Colin Powell and Condoleezza Rice to top ranks of policy elites—"as important as it is to improve racial equity in public service, these efforts do not automatically translate to fewer wars against predominantly black and brown countries, so long as the connection between race and foreign policy remains largely ignored." And, he wrote, "As we look inwards to dismantle America's legacy of racism that pervades the law enforcement and national security apparatuses, we must also recognize that racism and militarism are mutually reinforcing."[19]

✧

WHEN THE TENACIOUS INDEPENDENT journalist Nick Turse turned his attention to Africa early in this century's second decade, much to the dismay of the Pentagon's AFRICOM command, he refused to be stonewalled—and proceeded to shine light on shadowy operations by the U.S. military across the continent inhabited by more than a billion black people. American forces were running the gamut from joint military exercises to covert special ops, while U.S. media coverage hardly scratched the surface.

Sometimes, Turse discovered, the negative impacts on Africa have been indirect yet powerful. For example, when a military coup struck Burkina Faso in 2022 and deposed its democratically elected president, Turse provided key context. The man appearing on commandeered state television as the country's new leader, Lieutenant Colonel Paul-Henri Sandaogo Damiba, was "a highly trained soldier, thanks in no small part to the U.S. military, which has a long record of training soldiers in Africa who go on to stage coups," Turse wrote. "Damiba, it turns out, participated in at least a half-dozen U.S. training exercises, according to U.S. Africa Command."[20]

Between 2008 and 2022, the United States "pumped in more than $1 billion in security assistance to promote 'stability' in the region," Turse reported, while U.S.-trained officers "have attempted at least nine coups (and succeeded in at least eight) across five West African countries, including Burkina Faso (three times), Guinea, Mali (three times), Mauritania, and the Gambia." Training is just one component of the Pentagon's long-standing mission in West Africa. "Since the 2000s, the United States has regularly deployed small teams of commandos to advise, assist, and accompany local forces, even into battle; provided weapons, equipment, and aircraft."[21]

Those activities routinely occur in remote areas, under cloaks of secrecy, and little specific information about U.S. military partnerships or warfare in Africa seeps out. American citizens scarcely have a clue about what's being done with their tax dollars to fund military operations on the continent. That was the case when President Biden ordered the deployment of several hundred special operations forces to Somalia in mid-May 2022, eight months after telling the world that "for the first time in twenty years" the United States was "not at war" and had "turned the page." The *Washington Post* told readers that the Pentagon was reestablishing "a base of operations in Somalia" with a "small, persistent U.S. military presence."[22] It was a one-day news story.

Globally, the USA's clandestine military activities have no use for the informed consent of the governed back home. Democracy might just get in the way.

With little public scrutiny, eye-popping line items are larded into annual Pentagon appropriations before gliding through Congress and landing on the Oval Office desk for certain signature. Amid sparse and murky public information, the financing is profuse. "U.S. Special Operations Command has grown exponentially over the last twenty years," Turse explained in 2021, citing official figures. Specific funding for special operations "topped out at $3.1 billion in 2001, compared with $13.1 billion now. Before 9/11, there were roughly 43,000 special operations forces. Today, there are 74,000 military personnel and civilians in the command. Two decades ago, an average of 2,900 commandos were deployed overseas in any given week. That number now stands at 4,500."[23]

We're unlikely to ever get near the full story about the actual scope or human consequences of ongoing special ops. But Pentagon documents indicate that the secret operations are quite hazardous for participants. "As the command's global reach has grown, so has the toll on America's commandos," Turse reported for *The Intercept*. "While special operations forces make up just 3 percent of American military personnel, they have absorbed more than 40 percent of the casualties, mainly in conflicts across the Greater Middle East. Suicide rates among commandos are also the highest in the military and outpace the general population, according to an internal study of special operators' suicides between 2012 and 2015, commissioned by [U.S. Special Operations Command] and obtained by *The Intercept*. 'Nearly all cases suffered some form of PTSD or emotional trauma following the first deployment,' the report notes."[24]

How widely deployed are these special operations forces? As the century's third decade began, the Pentagon told Turse that the commandos were deployed in 141 countries.[25]

BEGINNING IN THE FINAL YEARS of the Obama presidency, an upsurge of activism started to emphasize vital connections. In 2022, a visitor to the homepage of the Movement for Black Lives website would find this on the first screen: "Since our founding in 2014, M4BL has successfully built significant cultural power; catalyzed growing opposition to white supremacy, patriarchy, militarism, and anti-Black racism; popularized intersectional Black feminism and the significance of anti-Black racism, Black spaces, and Black organizing."[26] Such an approach could do a lot to help dismantle the conceptual barriers that have separated crucial "issues" from each other.

While mainstream media took a dim view of drawing connections between repression at home and abroad, they were emerging with more clarity in many venues, including academia. At Johns Hopkins University, a professor of international relations, Robbie Shilliam, wrote that "what is clear is that racism should be conceived as both a domestic and a foreign-policy issue." And: "While the roots of the Movement for Black Lives are multiple and braided, they at least partially track what [W.E.B.] Du Bois understood to be the global color line. In the United States, Cold War and post–Cold War geopolitics have brought counterinsurgency strategies and militarized policing home to U.S. citizens—especially poor and the Black citizens."[27]

PEOPLE OF COLOR are at much higher risk of being shot dead by police than whites are—with a per-million population rate of forty-one for African Americans, twenty-nine for Hispanics, and sixteen for whites.[28] Bad as those statistics are, they only begin to convey how the policing and criminal justice systems mete out emotional and physical violence that is slanted by race. Millions of black boys and men are acutely aware of being unfair game for police harassment and brutality. Out of camera range and shielded from victims' redress, beatings are all too often inflicted by police officers with far more impunity than accountability. And behind the walls of the nation's jails and prisons, the power of guards to brutalize is infamous. Black people pay a hugely disproportionate price. "Black Americans are incarcerated in state prisons at nearly five times the rate of white Americans," a report by the Sentencing Project documented in 2021. "Nationally, one in eighty-one Black adults in the U.S. is serving time in state prison."[29]

Meanwhile, nationwide, police departments have continued to use weapons generously provided by the Pentagon. Undeterred by criticism of its "1033 program" supplying weaponry to local law enforcement agencies, the Defense Department transferred $850 million worth of military equipment to police across the country during the six years immediately after large sustained protests—in response to the fatal police shooting of teenager Michael Brown in Ferguson, Missouri—drew national attention in 2014. "Despite pledges from public officials including then president Barack Obama to review and restrict the program, the spigot of battlefield-caliber heavy equipment never stopped flowing," BuzzFeed News reported in 2020. That flow to police departments included "heavily armored personnel carriers, aircraft, ammunition, and other military equipment. While there are many ways for law enforcement agencies to acquire military-grade equipment, including outright purchases and grants, the 1033 program remains an important way for agencies to acquire big-ticket items at little to no cost."[30] News accounts told about transfers to police of more than thirteen thousand MRAPs—armored "Mine-Resistant Ambush Protected Vehicles"—which had been deployed in Afghanistan and Iraq.[31]

A week after the murder of George Floyd by a Minneapolis policeman in the late spring of 2020, *Wired* magazine described the scenes in many cities as anti-racism protesters were met by "police forces equipped with full body armor and tactical vehicles that vaguely resemble tanks. The local law enforcement responding to even nonviolent protests has often looked more like the U.S. Armed Forces." Militarization of police departments was cumulative—"over several decades, the 1033 program has shipped over $7.4 billion of Defense Department property to more than 8,000 law enforcement agencies."[32] Although the program got a bit of negative media notice when high-profile protests faced off against the Pentagon's donated equipment, its effects were ongoing. A Princeton professor specializing in police issues, Jonathan Mummolo, put it this way: "We tend to focus on these events when there's massive social unrest and they're dominating the headlines and we see militarized police come in, but militarized police are active in this country all the time."[33]

By the time Congressman Hank Johnson wrote a letter to President Biden in the spring of 2021, urging him to issue an executive order against the Pentagon's arming of police departments, Johnson had been unsuccessfully introducing bills along that line for seven years. "Decades of militarization of our nation's law enforcement have led to some police departments looking more like an occupying army than a community-based regulatory arm of state and local government," Johnson wrote. He added:

Law enforcement's response to the civil rights demonstrations last summer show irrefutable proof of our police forces' increasing aggression and brutality—images of local police in military vehicles, with military-grade weaponry trained on citizens exercising their constitutional right to peacefully protest. Studies have shown that the presence of military hardware in untrained hands increases the likelihood of negative outcomes. When a law enforcement officer is armed with a military-style weapon, they are simply more likely to use it. The inappropriate use of such weapons is incentivized by a perverse requirement that to keep the equipment transferred under the 1033 program, the receiving agency must utilize it within one year or it must be returned to DOD [Department of Defense]. This militarization of our police departments inherently decreases the trust that is crucial to the successful and necessary relationship between these agencies and the communities they are sworn to protect and serve. This program instead blurs the line between local police and an occupying military force.

Johnson's letter, cosigned by twenty-eight other House members, concluded: "Our neighborhoods need to be protected, including from dangers posed by the militarization of police."[34]

Thirteen months later, in May 2022, President Biden issued an executive order that set limits on the 1033 program but kept much of it intact.[35] A statement from Congressman Johnson said the order "included reforms" that would "stop the transfer of some of the most dangerous equipment."[36] Yet the federal pipeline of military weapons to local police forces around the country would continue.

Like some evolutionary technique of camouflage, fading into overall scenery, war weapons in the hands of police became less conspicuous as they became more ubiquitous.[37] Over time, deployed in the streets of the United States, they no longer would become recognizable as weapons of war but rather as equipment for policing that remains badly skewed against racial justice.

BECAUSE NO AMERICAN comes close to matching the stature of Martin Luther King Jr. as the nation's icon of struggles for racial justice, militarism continues to greatly benefit from the whitewashing of what he stood for—and eloquently spoke out for—in realms of foreign policy and war. Despite all the resulting denunciations of him, King "never refrained from harsh criticism of racism and imperialism," historian Brenda Gayle Plummer points out.[38] Speaking in mid-November 1967 at Britain's Newcastle University, where he received an honorary degree, King said: "There are three urgent and indeed great problems that we face not only in the United States of America but all over the world today. That is the problem of racism, the problem of poverty, and the problem of war, and the things that I have been trying to do in our struggle at home and in the struggle that is taking place all over the world has been to deal forthrightly and in depth with these great and grave problems that pervade our world."[39] The enumeration of racism, poverty, and war as urgent and overarching problems—far from being a laundry list of three disparate items— was a laser focus on intermeshed blights that were, then as now, tormenting humanity.

The connections that King so wisely drew have been mostly shredded in public discourse and political spheres. Poverty and near poverty in the United States are commonplace while

Pentagon budgets fatten. As for the other two great problems that King focused on—racism and war—the linkages that he stressed get scant attention. He was explicit in his "Beyond Vietnam" speech on April 4, 1967, as he advocated for "the shirtless and barefoot people" the world over. "Our only hope today," he said, "lies in our ability to recapture the revolutionary spirit and go out into a sometimes hostile world declaring eternal hostility to poverty, racism, and militarism."[40]

In the decades that followed, the same Democratic presidents fond of effusively revering the memory of King's leadership for civil rights had no use for his opposition to militarism, which makes sense since they were fully engaged in it. Meanwhile, the Congressional Black Caucus—founded and initially led in the 1970s by such stellar antiwar congressmembers as Shirley Chisholm, Ron Dellums, and John Conyers— gradually became part of the Capitol Hill apparatus for the military-industrial complex. The rainbow, multiracial presidential campaigns of Jesse Jackson in 1984 and 1988 included commitments to human rights and diplomacy instead of war, at a time when African Americans comprised the most antiwar demographic in the nation. A quarter century later, President Obama was crucial to making endless war bipartisan, and more acceptable to African American voters, as he picked up where his predecessor George W. Bush left off in Iraq, Afghanistan, and other parts of the globe.

In effect, the radically prophetic Martin Luther King was made nearly invisible by mass-mediated political discourse. From the ritualized tributes to King offered by elected officials and sizable media outlets, you'd never know what he had to say exactly a year before he was murdered. His "Beyond Vietnam" speech at Riverside Church in New York City was a thorough condemnation not only of the escalating war in Vietnam but also of what he called "the giant triplets of racism, extreme materialism, and militarism." The speech— which called the U.S. government "the greatest purveyor of violence in the world today"—was antithetical and infuriating to the nation's pro-war elites.[41]

King had gone down by the riverside, urging that his country study war no more. Then what happened? The editorial condemnations were fast and furious, from across the liberal-to-conservative media spectrum.[42] With a patronizing tone, the *Washington Post* warned that "King has diminished his usefulness to his cause, to his country, and to his people."[43] A *Newsweek* columnist accused King of wanting "a race-conscious minority" to dictate foreign policy.[44] *Life* magazine portrayed King as a communist tool who wanted "abject surrender in Vietnam" and was engaging in "demagogic slander that sounded like a script for Radio Hanoi."[45] Dropped from the national media's good graces, King was the equivalent of tarred, feathered, and run out of town. He continued to denounce the Vietnam War in categorical and multidimensional terms, while media vituperation was unrelenting.

After his death, a two-track approach to the martyred leader soon developed. Each year, on the anniversary of his death and later also on the Martin Luther King holiday, brief footage of his 1963 "I Have a Dream" speech might appear on television. As for his 1967 "Beyond Vietnam" speech, it went down a memory hole, not far from Orwellian territory, where U.S. news media almost never bothered to retrieve it. "The fact that most Americans know 'I Have a Dream' but not 'Beyond Vietnam' is testimony to the depth of American propaganda, the willingness of Americans to want to feel good about the American Dream and their reluctance to confront the American Nightmare," novelist Viet Thanh Nguyen wrote in 2020. "In the American Nightmare, the severity of anti-Black racism is inseparable from the endurance of American imperialism."[46]

Today, for the nation's media and political establishment, vehement denunciation of U.S. militarism and its interweave with domestic wrongs is no more welcome than during King's last year. Some styles have changed in media and politics, but war is still a bedrock of the country's economy and, perhaps less obviously, its culture. The ongoing contradictions between lofty rhetoric and actual military agendas, the conflicting messages from officials who urge prevention of lethal gun use in the United States while lauding the use of weapons to kill overseas—these and countless other disconnects give society a kind of moral and psychological whiplash.

One of the real-world boomerangs of indifference to destroying lives overseas is that, in the long run, wars do so much to undermine the lives of Americans at home. The U.S. military budget is still functioning much the way that King described it—as "some demonic, destructive suction tube."[47] As he said, "A nation that continues year after year to spend more money on military defense than on programs of social uplift is approaching spiritual death."[48] That was in 1967. So many decades later, the death rattles are unspeakably loud. Yet American society still has opportunities to willfully change how it truly values human lives, implementing new priorities via budgets as moral documents.

Now, questions rarely asked in the open are answered by militarized default. Such as: Who will count the costs of war? How does human life fit onto the ledger? How about the ecological toll, the social havoc, the anguish and trauma, the pain of physical agony and intimate grief? What are the calculations that assess how much death is "worth it"? Who gets to decide, and how, and does democracy really have anything to do with it? Who counts?

CHAPTER EIGHT

COSTS OF WAR

CONNECTIONS BETWEEN U.S. MILITARY ACTIVITIES IN OTHER countries and class conflicts at home get almost no media attention. Yet war's injuries to workers and their families are immense and multilayered, while war's profits for the wealthy and their families keep going through the roof. One cohort suffers grievous losses; the other posts enormous gains. The huge military budget—51 percent of all federal discretionary spending in 2022—sops up funds that could be devoted to health care, education, housing, job creation, and much more.[1] The poor, the near poor, and the barely middle class suffer most from the results. Meanwhile, untold physical and psychological harm is endured by those whom politicians are fond of calling—with proud emphasis on the second word of the phrase—"wounded warriors," preferring to acknowledge only the injuries to the body.

Very few of the rich went off to war while official Washington's appetite for invasions and other assaults grew from the morsels of Grenada and Panama in the 1980s to the much bigger geopolitical menus of the Middle East and beyond. The fat profit margins from supplying the Pentagon and kindred agencies with the tools of the imperial trade have been spoils of military war abroad as well as domestic class war—amid the steadily expanding gaps called "income inequality"; or, if you will, oligarchy.[2] During the twenty-first century, the thriving of the military-industrial-intelligence complex, embracing the tech sector with vast transactions, has meant gargantuan profits for elites while economic conditions have worsened or stayed precarious for most Americans.

In the real world of politics, financial power is political power. And, after all, successful politicians—elected officials—are the ones who decide whether, where, when, and how to go to war, as well as whether to escalate, scale down, or stop. If money was "the mother's milk of politics" when the aphorism emerged several decades ago, it now seems a quaint truism, perhaps more accurately phrased as "the heroin of politics." Analysis of contributions to key members of Congress for military outlays is to the point. For instance, Adam Smith. As the chair of the House Armed Services Committee, he was able to wield great power over appropriations for the Pentagon during 2022. For his successful reelection effort in 2020, his campaign committee and PAC had received upwards of $400,000 from military contractors.[3]

THE POET WILLIAM STAFFORD wrote that "every war has two losers."[4]

Yet war also brings immense rewards—advancing careers, boosting wealth, fueling profits. Even when the United States has ultimately lost a war in military and geopolitical terms, as in Vietnam and Afghanistan, some financial benefits have accrued to an extent that can be understated as gigantic.

The revenue—courtesy of the federal "defense" budget—has been well beyond human imagination in its magnitude.

And just as we cannot really fathom trillions of dollars, we probably can't fully grasp—no matter how hard we try—the dimensions of the partnerships between the U.S. military and corporations. Outfits like Lockheed Martin, Raytheon, General Dynamics, Boeing, and Northrop Grumman have never lost a war. Nor do they lose power. Hefty budgets for advertising, public relations, and lobbying always fortify images of civic responsibility and patriotism, while campaign contributions grease the big wheels.

For the firms guzzling from a Defense Department cornucopia to enlarge profits, the end use of the sold weaponry is almost beside the point. More direct impunity is conferred on the military chain of command. When news gets out about unjustifiable downsides of military actions, the media coverage has little staying power and little or no political impact. Accountability is close to nonexistent.

You could call it a kind of warlock's brew, with ingredients so thoroughly marinated together that they've become almost inseparable. It's difficult, maybe impossible to imagine the U.S. economy without massive military spending, or the country without warfare abroad or the (rarely noted) ongoing operations of some 750 U.S. military bases abroad.[5] During more than five decades since Martin Luther King decried "the madness of militarism,"[6] it has seeped and soaked and morphed deeper and deeper into the society, as wartime has become simply normal time; we really don't know how each facet could be extracted, removed from the mix of smells and tastes and textures that are now so familiar, blending into what can be a numbing or dopamine-inducing stew.

"Over the past ten years," National Priorities Project director Lindsay Koshgarian noted in 2021, "the U.S. has handed over $3.4 trillion (or $3.7 trillion in inflation-adjusted terms) to Pentagon contractors without headline-making congressional negotiations. It's part of the larger $7.2 trillion (2021 dollars) that we've handed over to Pentagon contractors almost unquestioned since 9/11." Along the way, taxpayers "heavily subsidized average CEO pay of $17.7 million at the top military contractors, and allowed corporations to rake in profits even while they failed wildly in the effort to reconstruct Afghanistan."[7]

The synergy between those who vote for a military budget and those who vastly profit from it has never been more powerful. "The arms industry has ample tools at its disposal to influence decisions over Pentagon spending going forward," William Hartung at the Center for International Policy wrote in late 2021. "The industry has spent $285 million in campaign contributions since 2001, with a special focus on presidential candidates, congressional leadership, and members of the armed services and appropriations committees in the House and Senate—the people with the most power over how much the country will spend for military purposes." And the largesse goes far beyond campaign donations, as Hartung documented in a report:

In addition, weapons makers have spent $2.5 billion on lobbying over the past two decades, employing, on average, over 700 lobbyists per year over the past five years, more than one for every member of Congress. The majority of these lobbyists have passed through the "revolving door" from jobs in Congress, the Pentagon, the National Security Council or other key agencies involved in determining the size and scope of the annual budget for national defense. . . . It's important to note that the revolving door swings both ways. Not only do former government personnel go into industry, but industry personnel frequently take influential positions in government.[8]

With that kind of pervasive leverage, no wonder corporate arms dealers have such a strong upper hand. At the same time, enormous incentives exist to avoid and deflect any reality check regarding what happens to human beings when the weaponry is used. The same interlocking systems that enrich war profiteers and shield them from scrutiny also avert clarity about faraway matters of life and death.

After two decades of the "war on terror," Brown University's Costs of War Project summarized[9] the human toll this way:

+ At least 929,000 people[10] have died due to direct war violence, including armed forces on all sides of the conflicts, contractors, civilians, journalists, and humanitarian workers.
+ Many times more have died indirectly in these wars, due to ripple effects like malnutrition, damaged infrastructure, and environmental degradation.
+ Over 387,000 civilians[11] have been killed in direct violence by all parties to these conflicts.
+ Over 7,050 U.S. soldiers[12] have died in the wars.
+ Many deaths and injuries among U.S. contractors[13] have not been reported as required by law, but it is likely that approximately 8,000 have been killed.[14]
+ 38 million people[15] have been displaced by the post-

9/11 wars in Afghanistan, Pakistan, Iraq, Syria, Libya, Yemen, Somalia, and the Philippines.

✦ The U.S. government is conducting counterterror activities in eighty-five countries, vastly expanding this war across the globe.[16]

In Washington, most elected Democrats join with Republicans in striving to paper over the true costs—individual, social, economic, environmental—of wars that they keep voting to fund.

AMONG THOSE WHO DIE on behalf of U.S. military interventions, few are less visible on the United States' political and media radar than the employees of private companies hired by the Pentagon and related agencies to do relatively high-paid—and high-risk—jobs in war zones. As with so many other aspects of the actual costs of war, what happens to those workers is neither a secret nor common knowledge. Media coverage is rare and political oversight is close to nonexistent. While news accounts and punditry might include figures on American casualties, those numbers have big holes in them. Officially, civilians on contracts don't count as casualties of war. And an unusual media spotlight on them quickly fades.

The *Washington Post* published a news article midway through 2020 under this provocative headline: "Use of Military Contractors Shrouds True Costs of War. Washington Wants It That Way, Study Says."[17] Citing research by Boston University and Brown University on "the commercialization of the post 9/11 wars,"[18] the newspaper reported that private

U.S. contractors in the Middle East were outnumbering U.S. troops there by 53,000 to 35,000. Since the autumn of 2001, an estimated 8,000 contractors had died in the region—"1,000 more than U.S. troops who have been killed." The scholar who coordinated the research, Heidi Peltier, said that the contractor system "hides the human cost and makes war more politically palatable."

Retired U.S. Army colonel Ann Wright told me that "MIC [military-industrial complex] contractors don't give a *shit* about their former employees." After twenty-nine years in the Army and Army Reserves, and after working as a State Department diplomat for sixteen years, Wright resigned in 2003 to protest the U.S. invasion of Iraq. Two decades later, she was vehement about the plights of civilian contractors, who have worked for hundreds of firms that raked in big profits.[19] "Virtually no one remembers the civilian contractors who in the final five-to-seven years of the war in Afghanistan outnumbered the U.S. military there," she said. "They were killed, wounded, taken hostage by the Taliban and militia forces."[20]

For the Defense Department, one of the advantages of hiring so many contractors has been that their deaths don't need to be announced or even acknowledged by the U.S. government. "If the death of a contractor occurs, the release of names and other information are handle[d] by the next of kin or the organization by which the individual was employed," a Pentagon spokesperson said.[21] Over the years, an increasing number of contractors have been hired to do traditional military tasks such as logistical functions, driving trucks, and staffing security shifts. In the aftermath of deaths or serious wounds, there is no access to veterans benefits, and survivors are left to the untender mercies of private employers, who often simply abandon them.

"The giant military no-bidding contractors like KBR, Halliburton, made billions of dollars but did *not* provide health care for employees after their individual contracts ended," Wright said. "So you have former employees all over the country who are suffering the same conditions for which military veterans receive some level of care from the VA—but civilian contractors and their families are left to fend for themselves."[22]

CONSTRAINED BY A UNIQUE system of laws, the Uniform Code of Military Justice, members of the armed forces are basically supposed to participate in warfare and be quiet if they don't agree with it. "When the U.S. military is a party to cases centering on First Amendment rights to free speech, free press, and free exercise of religion, the Supreme Court generally defers to the government's interest and discretion, permitting the military to restrict the rights of service personnel in ways it does not permit in civilian contexts," legal scholar Elizabeth Beaumont wrote. "The U.S. military has always operated as a somewhat distinct society governed by its own criminal code. . . . When responding to First Amendment challenges from military personnel, the Court consistently treats the military as a special and separate context or environment in which standard First Amendment protections do not apply, or do not apply to the same extent."[23] Ironically, while U.S. troops are often praised for helping to preserve American freedoms, the bedrock protections of the First Amendment are largely unavailable to them while in uniform.

Supreme Court chief justice Earl Warren commented in 1962 that "our citizens in uniform may not be stripped of basic rights simply because they have doffed their civilian clothes." But he toed the usual judicial line that sealed off conscripted as well as enlisted military personnel from the hazardous liberties of the First Amendment, concluding: "It is indisputable that the tradition of our country, from the time of the revolution until now, has supported the military establishment's broad power to deal with its own personnel. The most obvious reason is that Courts are ill-equipped to determine the impact upon discipline that any particular intrusion upon military authority might have."[24]

TRAUMATIC BRAIN INJURY (TBI) often afflicts Iraq and Afghanistan veterans who were violently jolted by explosions and other wartime events. Dozens of symptoms include painful, disorienting, and debilitating ordeals. "Mild traumatic brain injury may affect your brain cells temporarily," the Mayo Clinic explains, but more-serious TBI "can result in bruising, torn tissues, bleeding, and other physical damage to the brain. These injuries can result in long-term complications or death."[25] Citing Pentagon data, the Centers for Disease Control and Prevention flatly reported that "more than 450,000 U.S. service members were diagnosed with a TBI from 2000 to 2021."[26]

An in-depth study, released by the *Journal of Head Trauma Rehabilitation* in 2019, found that veterans who had suffered from TBI were more than twice as likely to commit suicide as other vets.[27] And suicide has been only one of many stealthy threats to veterans of this century's wars. In 2022, the American Medical Association's journal *JAMA* published a comprehensive study titled "Association of Traumatic Brain Injury with Mortality Among Military Veterans Serving After September 11, 2001." The findings identified numerous hazards: "Despite historically low combat fatality rates observed in Iraq and Afghanistan, our study suggests that post-9/11 military veterans face a higher mortality burden across multiple causes of death than the total U.S. population. We also found that exposure to moderate to severe TBI was associated with even higher mortality rates and excess mortality from accident, suicide, cancer, CVD [cardiovascular disease], homicide, and other causes." After two decades of war, the study concluded, "it is vital to focus attention on what puts veterans at risk for accelerated aging and increased mortality."[28]

WITHIN THE ARMED FORCES, the cultures of war are notably hazardous for women. "At every step toward their incorporation into the military," author Barbara Ehrenreich pointed out, "women have been met with coarse, misogynist resistance— jeers, hazings, and, above all, sexual assaults and harassment aimed at reminding them that, in the most primitive calculus, women are still not predators, but prey."[29] Ehrenreich wrote those words in the late 1990s. Twenty-five years later, they were not in the least outdated.

"For decades, sexual assault and harassment have festered through the ranks of the armed forces with military leaders repeatedly promising reform and then failing to live up to those promises," the *New York Times* reported in 2021. "Women remain a distinct minority, making up only 16.5 percent of the armed services, yet nearly one in four servicewomen reports experiencing sexual assault in the military, and more than half report experiencing harassment, according to a meta-analysis of sixty-nine studies published in 2018 in the journal *Trauma, Violence & Abuse*." Over the years of continuous warfare, the impacts of sexual assault within the ranks have measurably worsened. "From 2007 to 2017, the age-adjusted suicide rate among women veterans rose by 73 percent; according to Department of Defense data, in 2019, women accounted for 31 percent of all suicide attempts among active-duty service members."[30]

"Sexual assault in our military is an epidemic," Senator Kirsten Gillibrand said in 2021, "and it's clear that the current system is not working for survivors. Despite repeated efforts to protect our women and men in uniform, rates of harassment and assault continue to rise while prosecutions decline."[31] Months later, in December, clearly seething, Gillibrand issued a statement declaring that "House and Senate Armed Services leadership have gutted our bipartisan military justice reforms behind closed doors, doing a disservice to our service members and our democracy." She charged that the committee chairs (fellow Democrats) had blocked provisions to protect victims of sexual assault "in order to do the bidding of the Pentagon"—a statement that might cause us to ask why "the bidding of the Pentagon" would involve blocking protections for victims of sexual assault in the armed forces.[32]

Gillibrand voted against watered-down legislation, saying "this bill does not reform the military justice system in a way that will truly help survivors get justice" after sexual assault.[33] In early 2022, after signing the bill, President Biden issued an executive order as required by the new law, which made sexual harassment an "offense punishable" under the Uniform Code of Military Justice. "The move comes just a few weeks after lawmakers approved sweeping changes to how military sexual misconduct crimes are prosecuted," *Military Times* recounted.[34] But Gillibrand, the Senate's leading crusader against sexual assault in the military, was adamant that the "sweeping changes" were not anywhere near sweeping enough.

For decades, Pentagon officials have claimed a strict policy against sexual assault, much as they've claimed a strict policy of avoiding civilian deaths from military operations. In both cases, downplaying and covering up are standard operating procedures to reduce the visibility of the war system's victims. Sexual assault has remained an epidemic in the military because, among other reasons, it's consistent with the nation's war making. Use of overwhelming power to achieve desired ends is an ethos of the orders that come from the very top, no matter how much that operative ethos is prettied up with the formal authority of officialdom or pomp and circumstance. Objectifying "the other" is part of the training. A nation at nonstop war can hardly be expected to encourage sensitivity in the ranks.

"The first time I called 911 about my husband's violence was the second time it happened," Stacy Bannerman recounted. Her husband was a combat veteran with posttraumatic stress disorder (PTSD). "Before he came back from Iraq, I was given a military brochure that warned about irritability and hypervigilance, and instructed me to adjust to the 'new normal.' That I needed to adapt to this 'new normal' was echoed by VA personnel and TV programs. None of them mentioned that wives of veterans with PTSD are at a higher risk of severe domestic abuse and potentially lethal intimate partner violence than almost any other demographic in the nation, particularly if the veteran also has a traumatic brain injury."[35]

Bannerman almost died at the hands of her husband, who strangled her to the point of unconsciousness and threatened her with an M4 carbine assault rifle. She fled the marriage to save her life and went on to successfully call for—and then testify at—an unprecedented congressional hearing about domestic violence in the homes of returning war veterans. As the years of U.S. warfare went on, side effects of its overseas violence spiraled homeward with greater magnitude and intensity. What went around to Afghanistan and Iraq and other war zones came around to domestic lives.

"The past sixteen years have seen catastrophic rises in the rates of domestic violence, murder, and child abuse and neglect in families of post-9/11 veterans, evidenced by data from the Department of Justice, the Department of Veterans Affairs, and the Department of Defense," Bannerman wrote in 2017. "Before 9/11, the Army received roughly thirty-five to fifty cases of domestic abuse a month. By 2005, they were fielding approximately 143 cases a *week*, a twelve-fold increase. The Pentagon reported that there was also a demonstrable escalation in the severity of violence between 2001 and 2005. Calls to the National Domestic Violence Hotline from people affiliated with the military more than tripled[36] from 2006 to 2014."[37]

In 2022, the Veterans Administration was acknowledging a problem, while understating it with assessments like this: "Although IPV [intimate partner violence] affects all genders, one third of women veterans experience IPV in their lives compared to less than a quarter of civilian women."[38] Unofficial sources provide much more alarming data, which is to be expected; a 2021 audit by the Government Accountability Office concluded that the Defense Department was lax in collecting information on domestic violence.[39] The figures that the Pentagon did report indicated that physical violence was by far the most prevalent problem among veterans; the instances of domestic abuse were categorized as 74 percent physical, 22 percent emotional, and 4 percent sexual.[40]

The nonprofit Theresa's Fund—operating DomesticShelters. org as North America's largest directory of domestic violence programs and shelters—has provided a data summary. "Plenty of service members under some of the most stressful circumstances are not abusers," the organization noted. "However, servicemen and women do face additional challenges when it comes to escaping from or reporting abuse." What's more, abuse among military couples is "vastly underreported, as survivors often fear repercussions from their abuser should he or she be demoted as a result of reporting abuse."[41] The findings, titled "The Facts About Abuse in Military Families," should cause us to ponder long-term wartime effects on so many "wounded warriors" and those close to them.

+ Male combat veterans who suffer from PTSD are two to three times more likely to abuse their female partners than veterans not suffering from PTSD.
+ Among active-duty females, 36 percent report having experienced intimate partner violence during their service.
+ About 33 percent of combat veterans with PTSD report having been aggressive with their intimate partner at least once in the previous year.

✦ About 91 percent of combat veterans with PTSD
   reported being psychologically aggressive with their
   intimate partner in the previous year.

For those who endure the direct personal consequences
behind such numbers, there is nothing obscure or hidden
about them. For the rest of us, we're likely to never really
know.

And you wouldn't know it from news coverage or standard
political talk, but correlations between military training and
violence in U.S. society are not confined to private lives. The
impacts extend to the most deadly public uses of firearms.
"The facts speak for themselves," Hugh Gusterson, a professor of anthropology and international affairs at George
Washington University, wrote in 2016. While the proportion
of U.S. adults who were veterans averaged 13 percent during
recent decades,[42] "more than a third of the adult perpetrators
of the forty-three worst mass killings since 1984 had been in
the United States military. It is clear that, in the etiology of
mass killings, military service is an important risk factor."
He added that "we need research to illuminate the connection
between former military service and mass murder for the few
who snap."[43] Why does the connection exist? Gusterson out-
lined some of the factors. "There are obvious reasons why so
many mass killers might be military veterans. They may have
been drawn to the military in the first place by an attraction
to violence. Once in the military, they are trained in the art of
killing and, if they have combat experience, they may become
disinhibited from killing."[44]

✧

OVER TIME, HOME-FRONT enthusiasm for war tends to dissipate. It has proven to be especially difficult to sustain in working-class communities that have pervasive ongoing problems with economic scarcity, while experiencing the brunt of long-term impacts from direct participation in the nation's war efforts. For people of meager or modest means, compared to those in affluent sectors of society, what's involved with war—what scarcely comes through in media coverage, much less in the pronouncements of elected politicians and other public officials—looms much larger and deeper: hardships, pain, trauma, loss. Abstractions come much easier to those without family members or friends who've been deployed.

In his intuitively opportunistic way, while campaigning for president and then after taking office in early 2017, Donald Trump grasped the rhetorical openings that alienation offered. Americans who didn't feel they were being seen or heard included many who had firsthand, or just one degree of separation away from, experience with the visceral and cascading effects of being in armed forces at war. Trump could denounce warmongering yet also call for using maximal military force; almost in the same breath, he charged that Democrats were too willing to drag the country into wars or were too wimpy. He seemed to recognize what the decade and a half of war had meant to many Americans with few economic options. Albeit as a demagogue, Trump hit a nerve of truth; for many in the working class, the "war on terror" wasn't what it was cracked up to be.

The elitism that suffused Hillary Clinton's public image included her hawkish stance for war and more war. She seemed unable to project much empathy for what the wars, ostensibly being waged to protect America, were doing to

Americans, much less anyone else. (Some might guess that the closest she'd ever gotten to a working-class enterprise was during her six-year stint on Walmart's board of directors.) Her aloof relations with the working class were combined with what often appeared to be unabashed zeal for U.S. military engagements. By 2016, Clinton's persona of reflexive support for warfare left little room for connecting with American families who had soured on providing the personnel for endless war.

A conservative fellow at the libertarian Cato Institute, Doug Bandow, was among many commentators who lined up the pool shot against Hillary Clinton that fall. Six weeks before the general election, he used an angle that was right there on the table. Clinton, he wrote, "almost certainly would lead America into more foolish wars." For Bandow, a former special assistant to President Ronald Reagan, clarity about Clinton's highly distasteful predilections made Trump a much more palatable candidate: "Despite his many failings, he remains superior to Clinton when it comes to foreign policy. No one knows what Trump would do in a given situation, which means there is a chance he would do the right thing. In contrast, Clinton's beliefs, behavior, and promises all suggest that she most likely would do the wrong thing, embracing a militaristic status quo which most Americans recognize has failed disastrously." Bandow's article was published by *Forbes* under the headline "Hillary Clinton Never Met a War She Didn't Want Other Americans to Fight."[45] While very far from being genuine advocates for the working class, the likes of Bandow and *Forbes* recognized the widening gap between inside-the-Beltway fervor for war and what it was doing to many Americans shouldering the burdens of carrying it out.

✧

NO LONGER IN UNIFORM, veterans of the interminable "war on terror" have been eager to get on with their lives. Society could take the young adults out of the wars, but afterward it would be difficult to take the wars out of the young adults. Officials like to pretend that everyday people—making the nation's war machinery run on the ground, at sea, and in the air—can leave the military and return to civilian life not much the worse for wear. But for so many, what they experienced in the service of the Pentagon's war agenda was not a good fit for simply picking up where they'd left off. The disconnect could be too big a rift to bridge without a sense of alienation if not dissociation.

"It is not possible to fully unmake the soldier and remake the civilian if society will not honestly address the rationale of the current wars and their consequences," scholar Ellen Moore wrote in her 2017 book *Grateful Nation*. After several years of research including in-depth interviews with veterans, Moore concluded that official mental-health services, such as those provided by Vet Centers and the Veterans Administration, "are segregated spaces that generally do not involve conversations with non-military affiliated civilians, and they do not involve conversations with the broader civilian society. Discussions with and among veterans usually take place behind closed doors. At Vet Centers, the psychological treatment model is based on the philosophy that veterans can best be helped by military peers. The implication of this model is that it is counter-therapeutic to have conversations with civilians about the realities of war."[46]

Whatever its therapeutic value might be, that model makes candid communication about veterans' actual wartime experiences largely off-limits for sharing with civilians and society as a whole. Yet the ripple—and sometimes grimly cascading—effects of those experiences are hardly a secret to veterans and their loved ones. The lasting impacts are apt to compound the pressures and anxieties common to adult life, with financial difficulties often a key part of the mix. All told, veterans and their families have ample reasons to believe that the importance of their lives—made more stressful and sometimes anguished by participation in war efforts—is being routinely devalued; they're not really being seen.

Emotions of feeling discounted might seem too subtle or personal for seasoned politicos to take very seriously, but there can be electoral consequences. During the 2016 presidential campaign, the wisdom of continual war was far clearer to the Democratic nominee than it was to voters in areas most familiar with combat deaths, injuries, multiple tours of duty, and psychological traumas. Research data from voting patterns in pivotal swing states suggested that the Clinton campaign's pro-war image was a political detriment in working-class communities hard-hit by results of deployments in Iraq and Afghanistan.[47] "Even controlling in a statistical model for many other alternative explanations, we find that there is a significant and meaningful relationship between a community's rate of military sacrifice and its support for Trump," concluded a study by Boston University's Douglas Kriner and Francis Shen at the University of Minnesota. The professors wrote, "Our statistical model suggests that if three states key to Trump's victory—Pennsylvania, Michigan, and Wisconsin—had suffered even a modestly lower casualty rate, all three could have flipped from red to blue and sent Hillary Clinton to the White House." In their study, Kriner and Shen said that Democrats might want to "reexamine their foreign policy posture if they hope to erase Trump's electoral gains among constituencies exhausted and alienated by fifteen years of war."[48]

WHILE AMERICANS ON LOW and middle rungs of the economic ladder have long been slipping under financial pressure, the prospects for young people have been hit particularly hard. Even before the COVID-19 pandemic, Pew Research data showed, the phenomenon of young and not-so-young adults living with their parents had been on a steep rise from the beginning of this century.[49] By the time President Biden took office, 30 percent of current and former college attendees—45 million borrowers—were burdened with a total of $1.7 trillion in student debt;[50] the average totaled upwards of $38,000.[51]

Meanwhile, entry-level jobs usually looked unenticing. "Work at the low end of the wage scale has become ghastly over the past several decades," the *American Prospect* executive editor David Dayen wrote in 2021. "With no meaningful improvements in federal labor policy since the 1930s, employers have accrued tremendous power. . . . Low-wage employers rely on an endless reserve of desperate workers willing to break their backs for a pittance."[52]

When targeted for recruitment into the military, young people might feel they don't have other passable options. Offering alternatives to unpleasant civilian conditions, military recruiters promise that enlisting means opening doors to better opportunities.

Yet the chronic budget priorities of colossal pork for the Pentagon and interlocked behemoths have much to do with the longtime downturn of social mobility. Military spending dollar for dollar is one of the least efficient ways to create and sustain employment.[53] "Federal spending on domestic programs creates far more American jobs and yields more broad-based benefits than military spending," a Brown University study found. For instance, the research documented that "investments in elementary and secondary education create nearly three times as many American jobs as defense spending, while health care creates about twice as many jobs."[54]

The working class and the middle class, however defined, would greatly benefit if much of the present-day Pentagon spending went to domestic public investment. But the ballooning military budgets sustain priorities to lift an array of corporate megaprofits. Whether they know it or not, young people "in the service" are functioning in the service of those priorities.

"War is a class conflict, too," Alexandria Ocasio-Cortez tweeted after a year in the House of Representatives. "The rich and powerful who open war escape the consequences of their decisions. It's not their children sent into the jaws of violence." She added: "It is often the vulnerable, the poor, & working people—who had little to no say in conflict—who pay the price."[55]

But no such concerns were in evidence when Defense Secretary Lloyd Austin spoke at the Reagan National Defense Forum on December 4, 2021. "Let me tell you about some steps that we're taking to transform the way that we do business," he said, before outlining a vision of partnerships: "First, we're paving new pathways for American innovators and entrepreneurs to work with us. Consider the Defense

Advanced Research Projects Agency—better known as DARPA. It is legendary for scientific breakthroughs. But now, DARPA is also connecting its top research teams with corporate leaders and U.S. investors so that those teams can build successful businesses with the cutting-edge technologies that they develop."

The Pentagon chief sketched out a future when educators, big-time investors, and inventive minds will be working even more closely with the military. "We're also doing more to integrate the [Defense] Department's innovators into tech hubs around the country where academics, and business leaders, and innovators thrive," he said, adding that a crucial goal was to "quickly see if promising tech and prototypes can help our warfighters."[56]

AS JOE BIDEN'S PRESIDENCY unfolded, Donald Trump's lockstep allies in Congress were perfectly comfortable hitching the wagons of their solipsistic political careers to someone with contempt for any and all inconvenient facts. Prospects for more power trumped other considerations. At first glance, such dynamics seem unrelated to the nonstop wars that were in their sixteenth year by the time Trump entered the White House. On closer examination, the intersections run deep.

The military—especially in times of war—is the most authoritarian major institution in American society, with the exception of jails and prisons. The command structure is rigid and virtually uncontestable. Meanwhile, whatever rules of war may exist, and whatever lip service is provided to them, in actual practice during combat they might count for little—

especially when no one is looking. An operative precept is: whatever works. Trump's electoral successes, including his intimidation of congressional Republicans afraid to cross him even after he left office, attested to shrewd dedication to doing whatever he could get away with to achieve his objectives. With thresholds of acceptability declining in domestic political life, the Trump frenzy came more and more to resemble the mentalities of warfare.

The raison d'être of war is to achieve goals with violence—the central approach of the pro-Trump mob that breached the Capitol on January 6, 2021, in a desperate attempt to prevent Joe Biden from becoming president. The insurrectionists, exhibiting loyalty to the man at the top of the command structure, escalated to violence when all else had failed. Many of the mob's de facto leaders drew on training acquired while in the U.S. military. After researching the backgrounds of prominent attackers who'd been swiftly arrested, NPR News reported—under the headline "Military Veterans Overrepresented in Those Charged in January 6 Capitol Riot"—that "nearly 1 in 5 people charged over their alleged involvement in the attack on the U.S. Capitol appear to have a military history."[57] (At the time, only 7 percent of adults in the United States were military veterans.[58]) The headline over an Associated Press story was telling: "The War Comes Home: Capitol Mob Included Highly Trained Ex-Military and Cops."[59]

Indictments of the assault's key leaders underscored military backgrounds.[60] A year after the attack on the Capitol, when eleven organizers of the Oath Keepers militia were indicted on sedition charges stemming from their January 6 roles, it turned out that five of them—including the head of the group, Elmer Rhodes—were military veterans.[61] Later, in June 2022, four out of the five Proud Boys leaders indicted for seditious conspiracy in the Capitol siege were veterans. Military.com reported that "the indicted men include an Army combat veteran with a Purple Heart, two Marines who served in the infantry and logistics, and a sailor recruit who washed out in boot camp."[62]

By mid-2022, federal charges had been filed accusing 835 individuals of involvement in storming the Capitol. George Washington University's Program on Extremism found that "at least" 13 percent of them had "military experience"—double the national average for adults.[63]

The fact that the Joint Chiefs of Staff chairman was highly alarmed at the possibility of Trump attempting to seize power in January 2021 does not negate another reality: Trump was drawing on a deeply militaristic cultural mentality, fueled by nearly twenty years of nonstop war at that point; the "training" of his militant and dangerous supporters was most importantly about mindsets. Trump was, after all, the "commander in chief." And the might-makes-right approach of U.S. warfare overseas was fully compatible with the behavior of his most violent backers at the Capitol. The complete legitimization of war as a 24/7/365 decades-long part of America's national identity has stoked feverish beliefs that politics can be domestic war by other means. And vice versa.

THE FIRST TWO DECADES of the century normalized war as an ongoing American way of life. President Obama seemed to be alluding to such reality early in his second term, when he spoke at the National Defense University and declared: "Our systematic effort to dismantle terrorist organizations must continue. But this war, like all wars, must end. That's what history advises. That's what our democracy demands."[64] It was a grand statement, exciting to liberal-minded journalists like Jane Mayer, who promptly wrote in the *New Yorker*— under the overblown headline "Obama's Challenge to an End-less War"—about the president's "anguish over the difficult trade-offs that perpetual war poses to a free society." She added, "Obama appears somewhat unsure of exactly what actions to take. That is not a bad thing: at least he is asking the right questions. In fact, by suggesting that, after a decade and seven thousand American and countless foreign lives lost, and a trillion dollars spent, it might be time to start down-sizing the 'war on terror,' he is leading the national debate beyond where even most Democrats have dared to go."[65]

Obama's occasional musings about the demands of democ-racy to limit perpetual war indicated that he was aware of some negative effects on U.S. society. Unfortunately, he didn't seem to care enough to do much about it. During the forty-four months that followed his National Defense Uni-versity speech, until leaving office, Obama did not lead a national debate much of anywhere. From 2013 through 2016, the United States maintained the bombing of Afghanistan at about half the rate of his first term while drastically esca-lating the attacks in Iraq and Syria, with 30,743 bombs and missiles dropped on those two countries in 2016 alone.[66] In truth, Obama's two terms did little to de-emphasize militaris-tic mindsets and much to reinforce them.

A central theme of Joe Biden's 2020 presidential campaign was this warning: "If we give Donald Trump eight years in the White House, he will forever alter the character of our nation."[67] Left unasked and unaddressed was a profoundly important question: To what extent had nearly twenty years of nonstop war altered the character of the nation?

Is the United States truly in the grip of "the madness of militarism"? Certainly not everyone and certainly not everywhere. Yet, overall, the country is gripped by war's dispersed and often private consequences—the aggravated tendencies toward violence, the physical wartime injuries, the post-traumatic stress, the profusion of men who learned to use guns and were trained to shoot to kill when scarcely out of adolescence, the role modeling from recruitment ads to popular movies to bellicose bombast from high-ranking leaders, and much more. The country is also in the grip of tragic absences: the health care not deemed fundable by those who approve budgets larded with military spending, the child care and elder care and family leave not provided by those same budgets, the public schools and higher education deprived of adequate funding, the gaping holes in social safety nets, the uncountable other everyday deficits that have continued to lower the bar of the acceptable and the tolerated.

Echoing Ralph Waldo Emerson, we could say that wars are in the saddle of America, locked into stirrups. The reasons for war have over time come to include war itself—going on because it is already going on. As Barbara Ehrenreich has written, "However and wherever war begins, it persists, it spreads, it propagates itself through time and across space with the terrifying tenacity of a beast attached to the neck of living prey. This is not an idly chosen figure of speech. War spreads and perpetuates itself through a dynamic that often seems independent of human will. It has, as we like to say of things we do not fully understand, 'a life of its own.'"[68]

CHAPTER NINE

NOW IT CAN BE TOLD

President Bush has said Iraq has weapons of mass destruction. Tony Blair has said Iraq has weapons of mass destruction. Donald Rumsfeld has said Iraq has weapons of mass destruction. Richard Butler has said they do. The United Nations has said they do. The experts have said they do. Iraq says they don't. You can choose who you want to believe.

—ARI FLEISCHER, WHITE HOUSE
PRESS SECRETARY, DECEMBER 5, 2002[1]

Well, if you are just digesting Russian misinforma-tion and parroting Russian talking points, you are not aligned with longstanding bipartisan American values, which is to stand up for the sovereignty of countries like Ukraine but others, their right to choose their own alliances and also to stand against, very clearly, the efforts or attempts or potential attempts by any country to invade and take territory of another country.

—JEN PSAKI, WHITE HOUSE
PRESS SECRETARY, FEBRUARY 2, 2022[2]

AS THE IRAQ INVASION NEARED IN EARLY 2003, MAJOR NEWS
outlets choked off access to debate.[3] Longtime TV eminence
Phil Donahue was leading MSNBC's prime-time ratings with
his show when the network pulled the plug just three weeks
before the invasion began. A leaked internal memo explained
the concerns of top management that Donahue's program represented a "difficult public face for NBC in a time of war." The
memo added, "He seems to delight in presenting guests who
are anti-war, anti-Bush and skeptical of the administration's
motives." The document warned that the show could become
"a home for the liberal anti-war agenda at the same time that
our competitors are waving the flag at every opportunity."[4]
MSNBC was eager to be on the right side of the flag-waving,
so Donahue had to go before the shooting started.

By early in the Biden presidency's second year, spokespeople had gotten into a nasty habit of casting aspersions on
those asking tough questions about foreign affairs. And so, at
a State Department news conference, when asked by an Associated Press reporter for any evidence to back up claims that
Russia was planning a "false flag" operation to justify invading Ukraine, government spokesman Ned Price bristled at the
journalist's persistence and then snapped: "If you doubt the
credibility of the U.S. government, of the British government,
of other governments and want to, you know, find solace in
information the Russians are putting out, that is for you to
do."[5]

When *Mother Jones* published an article headlined "Why
Are Biden's Spokespeople Being All Authoritarian?" the sub-
head was apt: "The suggestion that questioning government

claims is disloyal has to stop."[6] Even some journalists hardly known for polarizing with authorities found the emerging pattern disturbing enough to speak out. Longtime NPR *Morning Edition* host Steve Inskeep responded after an NPR colleague asked the White House press secretary what Inskeep called "a basic, fundamental, professional question reporters commonly ask of anyone." He tweeted: "To reply 'believe me, or believe ISIS' is not an answer. This country has tried war on the 'You're with us or against us' model, and it didn't work then either."[7]

During a news briefing, White House press secretary Jen Psaki had been disparagingly impatient when NPR News correspondent Ayesha Rascoe asked about the Pentagon's account of a U.S. attack that had just killed an ISIS leader along with ten women and children in Syria. After Rascoe asked a reasonable question, the exchange quickly rolled downhill:

Q: With regard to the civilian casualties in Syria, are—is the administration saying that they were caused entirely by the bomb detonating or by crossfire from the one lieutenant engaging with U.S. forces? Like, what—give us some clarity on that.

PSAKI: Obviously, these events just happened overnight. And so, I'm going to let the Department of Defense do a final assessment, which I'm certain they will provide additional detail on once it's finalized.

Q: Jen, will there be any, like, evidence or, like, release to support the idea—I mean, I know the U.S. has put out its statement that, you know, they detonated the bomb themselves. But will the U.S. provide any evidence? Because there may be people that are skeptical

of the events that took place and what happened to
the civilians.

PSAKI: Skeptical of the U.S. military's assessment when
they went and took out an ISIS terror—the leader of
ISIS?

Q: Yes.

PSAKI: That they are not providing accurate information—

Q: Yes.

PSAKI: —and ISIS is providing accurate information?

Q: Well, not ISIS, but, I mean, the U.S. has not always
been straightforward about what happens with civilians. And, I mean, that is a fact.[8]

After two decades of the "war on terror," for those paying attention, the U.S. government's credibility had badly
corroded. After incalculable harm had been done, the belated
telling of partial truths by politicians and media outlets frequently involved not only convenient amnesia about the
extent of previous pro-war deceptions but also fatuous claims
about the past, for example the enduring U.S. media myth
that everyone thought Iraq had weapons of mass destruction
before the invasion.[9]

Such revisionism is more than just reluctance to admit terrible mistakes of judgment and advocacy. It also has an effect
of continuing to sequester and marginalize, in the shadows,
antiwar voices—thus making warfare's carnage seem akin to
unavoidable, as if the war had not been a choice as much as
merely an honest mistake.

✦

TIMING IS CRUCIAL in media and politics—and never more so than when war is at stake. It's completely unsatisfactory for journalists to toe the war line for years and then finally report, in effect: *Now it can be told—years too late.*

Virtually the entire U.S. media establishment gave full-throated support to the U.S. attack on Afghanistan in early October 2001. Twenty years later, many of the same outlets were saying the war was ill-conceived and doomed from the start. Immediately after the invasion of Iraq began in March 2003, with very few exceptions, even the mainstream news organizations that had been expressing trepidation or opposition swung into line to support the war effort. Two decades later, many of the same media outlets were calling the invasion of Iraq the worst U.S. foreign policy blunder in history.

But such framing evades the structural mendacity that remains built into the military-industrial complex, with its corporate media and political wings. War is so normalized that its casualties, as if struck by acts of God, are routinely viewed as victims without victimizers, perhaps no more aggrieved than people suffering the consequences of bad weather. What American policy makers call mistakes and errors are, for others, more aptly described with words like "catastrophes" and "atrocities." Attributing the U.S. wars to faulty judgment—not premeditated and hugely profitable aggression—is expedient, setting the policy table for supposed resolve to use better judgment next time rather than challenging the presumed prerogative to attack another country at will.

When the warfare in Afghanistan finally ended, major U.S. media—after avidly supporting the invasion and then the occupation—were awash in accounts of how the war had been badly run, with ineptitude or deception from the White

House and the Pentagon. Some of the analysis and commentaries might have seemed a bit sheepish, but news outlets preferred not to recall their prior support for the same war in Afghanistan that they were now calling folly.

A pattern of regret (not to say remorse) emerged from massive U.S. outlays for venture militarism that failed to triumph in Afghanistan and Iraq, but there is little evidence that the underlying repetition compulsion disorder has been exorcized from America's foreign policy leadership or mass media, let alone its political economy. On the contrary: the forces that have dragged the United States into making war in numerous countries still retain enormous sway over foreign and military affairs. For those forces, over time, shape-shifting is essential, while the warfare state continues to rule.

The fact that strategies and forms of intervention are evolving, most notably in the direction of further reliance on airpower rather than ground troops, makes the victims of the USA's firepower even less visible to American eyes. This presents a challenge to take a fresh look at ongoing militarism and insist that the actual consequences for people at the other end of U.S. weaponry be exposed to the light of day—and taken seriously in human terms.

Despite all that has happened since President George W. Bush vowed in mid-September 2001 to "rid the world of the evil-doers," pivotal issues have been largely dodged by dominant U.S. media and political leaders.[10] The toll that red-white-and-blue militarism takes on other countries is not only a matter of moral principles. The United States is also in jeopardy.

That we live in one interdependent world is no longer debatable. Illusions about American exceptionalism have been conclusively refuted by the global climate emergency and the COVID-19 pandemic, along with the ever-present and worsening dangers of thermonuclear war.[11] On a planet so circular in so many ways, what goes around comes around.

IN ONE MEDIA NARRATIVE, the suffering of the invaded was unfortunate yet secondary. In another media narrative, the suffering of the invaded was heart-wrenching and profound.

What began on March 20, 2003, in Iraq and on February 24, 2022, in Ukraine set off horrendous fear, anguish, pain, and death in those countries. No real difference in human terms. The decisions from the White House and the Kremlin, accompanied by profusely deceptive rhetoric, were of comparable moral decency: none. The people living in the two invaded countries endured similar experiences. But in the United States, the responses were worlds apart.

In the immediate and long aftermaths of the Iraq invasion, the standard outlook from within the United States was through a glass darkly. While the lives of American troops loomed large, the others were out of focus or unseen, minimally worthy of concern, much less grief. The suffering of people in Iraq would have to be imagined, since there was precious little of it intelligibly presented for viewing or hearing via the usual media outlets or conveyed by leaders in Washington. During the invasion and for the years afterward—on television or radio, in print, or on the screens of devices, in a wartime zeitgeist that was for most Americans scarcely wartime at all—Iraqis appeared as a sporadic series of fleeting and flickering images, not more tangibly part of human reality than any number of other constellations of pixels. The invasion of Iraq was mainly about the United States, about *us*. The steady flow of narratives, whether from the White House, State Department, and Capitol Hill, or directly from media outlets, was constant reinforcement of default belief in the centrality of American existence as a—as *the*—light onto the world; "American exceptionalism" with an inexhaustible supply of energy. In such a political and social environment, how real could Iraqi people seem?

Prompted by intensive messaging from media and their own government, Americans understood that Ukrainian people were fully deserving of sympathy, deep concern, support. Two decades earlier, Iraqi people had been just as deserving, but their ordeals—if depicted at all—were easily slotted into categories of difficult-to-prevent vicissitudes of war, especially as their suffering was due to the armed forces of a government reflexively assumed to be well-meaning. Indefensible transgressions, such as exposed murders of civilians or sadistic tortures at Abu Ghraib prison near Baghdad, were officially treated as anomalies rather than indices, and as PR problems for the United States in the Arab world.[12]

Only rarely did photos from U.S. torture sessions emerge into public view. Grisly descriptions gradually surfaced in the press, but they had little media staying power and mostly ended up swept under the political rug. President Obama acknowledged at an August 2014 news conference, "We tortured some folks." And he added, "When we engaged in some of these enhanced interrogation techniques, techniques that I believe and I think any fair-minded person would believe were torture, we crossed a line."[13] But after winning the presidency, Obama had swiftly made clear that he wouldn't dwell on such Bush-era crimes. On the eve of his inauguration, he declared about torture: "We need to look forward as opposed to looking backwards."[14] It was a way of saying that the torture—and the people who were tortured—should not be taken too seriously.[15]

THE WAR THAT FOLLOWED the invasion of Iraq, inflicting unimaginable violence, included large-scale massacres such as the 2004 assaults on Fallujah that received woefully sparse notice in the United States;[16] the scope and systemic brutality of the U.S. war in Iraq were seldom grasped back home. Through it all, in the United States' mainstreams of media and politics, any suggestion that some top U.S. officials might be appropriately charged with war crimes was assumed to be far outside the bounds of reasonable discussion.

Yet just days after the Russian invasion of Ukraine, accusations of "war crimes" were common in U.S. media. And news outlets were quick to laud antiwar protesters in Russia. In sharp contrast, by the time the invasion of Iraq got underway, antiwar protesters in the United States drew little media coverage and at that point were often targets of scorn for supposed failure to "support the troops."

My longtime colleague Jeff Cohen, who worked as a senior producer at MSNBC during the run-up to the invasion of Iraq, closely monitored the content of U.S. television networks in early 2022 as war in Ukraine went from a danger to a reality. Despite decades as a media analyst and professor of journalism, he was stunned by the one-eighty disparity in media treatment of the two invasions. "While covering Russia's horrific aggression in Ukraine, there is a real focus—as there always should be—on civilian victims of war," he wrote. "Today, the focus on that essential aspect of the Russian invasion is prominent and continuous—from civilian deaths to the trauma felt by civilians as missiles strike nearby. Unfortunately, there was virtually no focus on civilian death and agony when it was the U.S. military launching the invasions."[17]

Cohen has long been a voracious consumer of TV news, with a daily routine of watching several hours of cable channels and evening newscasts on the biggest networks. The counterpoints between invasions kept blowing his mind. As he put it, "In coverage of Russia's invasion of Ukraine, U.S. mainstream media have correctly, repeatedly, and without equivocation, invoked international law and declared it illegal. As they did when Russia invaded Crimea in 2014. By contrast, when the U.S. illegally invaded or attacked country after country in recent decades, international law has almost never been invoked by mainstream U.S. media. That was surely the case in the lead-up to the Iraq invasion."

Without a single standard of human rights and empathy for the victims of war, we lose human connection with them. And with ourselves.

ON A WARM AUTUMN afternoon in 2021, I sat with Daniel Ellsberg on the deck next to his house. The San Francisco Bay shimmered off in the distance behind him. Fifty years had passed since Ellsberg—risking prison for the rest of his life—provided the *New York Times* and other newspapers with seven thousand pages of top-secret documents that quickly became known as the Pentagon Papers. From then on, he continued to speak, write, and protest as a tireless antiwar activist.

I asked what the impacts would likely be if pictures of people killed by the U.S. military's bombing were on the front pages of American newspapers.

"I am in favor, unreservedly, of making people aware what the human consequences are of what we're doing— where we are killing people, what the real interests appear to be involved, who is benefiting from this, what are the circumstances of the killing," Ellsberg replied. "I want that to come out. It is not impossible, especially in nowadays of social media, where people can be their own investigative journalists and they can get it out and so forth. Where I have been somewhat disillusioned is not to think that can't help, but to be aware it's very far from being a guarantee that anything will change. There's no question that the media, like the government, collaborates in keeping this from the awareness and the attention—and that, to some extent, is surely to the credit of the American people, who are surely less responsible having been lied to, than the ones doing the lying. But why were they lied to? How much would they do if they weren't lied to?"

Ellsberg talked about differences between media coverage of 9/11 and, later, the U.S. military's "shock and awe" missile attack on Baghdad that began the Iraq invasion. In response to the horrors of September 11, he recalled, the *New York Times* "did something very dramatic. They ran a picture, a head picture, of each person who had been killed—with some anecdotes from their neighbors, their friends, and their family. This person liked to skydive, or this person liked to play in a band, or little anecdotes about what made them human, what people remembered about them in particular, very gripping, very moving."

After the Iraq War began, Ellsberg said, he thought: "Imagine if the *Times* were to run a page or two of photographs of the people who burned on the night of 'shock and awe.' . . . It wouldn't be that hard, if you were on the ground, we weren't then but we were later, to find the people who were relatives of those people. And say, look, each one had friends, had parents, had children, had relatives—each one had made their mark in some little way in the world until that moment when they were killed—and these were the people we killed, and these were the people who were dying under the bombing, exactly as in our case, where two planes filled with gas burned two buildings." But such U.S. media coverage was unthinkable. "Of course it's never happened—nothing like it."

Looking back at patterns of American attitudes toward war deaths, Ellsberg was not optimistic: "It's fair to say, as a first approximation, that the public doesn't show any effective concern for the number of people we kill in these wars. At most, they are concerned about the American casualties, especially if they're too many. They will put up, to an almost surprising degree, [with] a considerable level of American casualties, but especially if they're going down and especially if the president can claim success in what he was trying to do. But in terms of people killed in the course of that, the media don't really ask the question, the public doesn't ask the question of the media, and when it does come out, one way or another, occasionally, nothing much changes."

What is concealed from Americans, he went on, "is that they are citizens of an empire, they are in the core of an empire that feels itself as having the right to determine who governs other countries, and if we don't approve of them because of their effect on corporate interests, or their refusal to give us bases, or through pipelines of a kind that we need, we feel absolutely right and capable of removing them, of regime change."

Ellsberg added, "Virtually every president tells us, or reassures us, that we are a very peace-loving people, very slow to go to war, very reluctant, perhaps too slow in some cases, but very determined once we're in, but it takes a lot to get us to accept the idea of going to war, that that's not our normal state. That of course does go against the fact that we've been at war almost continuously. . . . That there is deception, that the public is evidently misled by it early in the game, in the approach to the war, in a way that encourages them to accept a war and support a war, is the reality. How much of a role does the media actually play in this, in deceiving the public, and how difficult is it to deceive the public? I would say, as a former insider, one becomes aware: it's not difficult to deceive them. First of all, you're often telling them what they would like to believe—that we're better than other people, we are superior in our morality and our perceptions of the world."

SPEAKING TO AN AMERICAN LEGION annual conference as the Democratic presidential nominee in 2016, Hillary Clinton pressed the credo of exceptionalism into heavy use. "Much of the speech focused on the idea of 'American exceptionalism,' which broadly refers to the view that the United States was created differently than other nations and bears singular global responsibilities," the *Washington Post* reported.[18] There was no ambiguity as Clinton held forth at the podium. "Part of what makes America an exceptional nation is that we are also an indispensable nation," she said. "In fact, we are *the* indispensable nation. People all over the world look to us and follow our lead."[19]

The president at the time, Barack Obama, was on the same declamatory page. From the bully pulpit, he often explained that the world could not do without the United States of America in the lead. Typical of such oratory was his West Point commencement speech in 2014, when he proclaimed: "The United States is and remains the one indispensable nation. That has been true for the century passed and it will be true for the century to come."[20]

It will be true for the century to come. How to account for such a declaration from the most powerful person in the world? Hubris? Calculated hyperbole? Jingoistic pandering? Nationalistic megalomania? Machismo? All of the above? Whatever the conceits, they can be made transparent by stripping away the finery that clothes naked self-interest, aggrandizement, and massive profit-taking from weapons sales as well as international leverage for economic gain and geopolitical positioning. The bottom line is that—as an "indispensable nation"—the United States is indispensable to itself.[21]

"Our society has spent so much time and has achieved such startling results with the discovery of new mechanical processes of communication," said theatrical director Lee Strasberg, "but we have somehow forgotten that the process of living demands the ability to respond, to make contact, and to communicate one's experience to another human being."[22] Likewise, what about the unrealized potential to truly receive communication and to empathize with the experiences of other human beings, far away, in drastically different circumstances, even when—especially when—made dire and worse by our own country's actions? The myths wrapped up in concepts like "American exceptionalism" cut against such possibilities. Along the way, to the extent we can't see the other as human, we become less.

"It is, of course, in the very nature of a myth that those who are its victims and, at the same time, its perpetrators, should, by virtue of these two facts, be rendered unable to examine the myth, or even to suspect, much less recognize, that it is a myth which controls and blasts their lives," James Baldwin wrote.[23] In its third decade of continuous war, in the name of fighting terror, propelled by military might and mythology about extraordinary virtues, the United States has become its own enemy. Meanwhile, the USA's unrelenting global search for enemies has made them more numerous and intractable. Now, an imperative is to insist on telling vital truths and acting on them. As Baldwin saw, "Not everything that is faced can be changed; but nothing can be changed until it is faced."[24]

NOTES

INTRODUCTION

1. "The American Offensive Begins," *New York Times*, October 8, 2001.
2. Steve Rendall, "Journalists Gaga for 'Rock Star' Rumsfeld," Fairness and Accuracy In Reporting, March 1, 2002, www.fair.org/home /journalists-gaga-for-rock-star-rumsfeld.
3. Rendall, "Journalists Gaga."
4. Rendall, "Journalists Gaga."
5. Loretta Alper and Jeremy Earp, directors, *War Made Easy* (Media Education Foundation, 2007), documentary film.
6. Carl Conetta, "Operation Enduring Freedom: Why a Higher Rate of Civilian Bombing Casualties," Project on Defense Alternatives, January 18, 2002, www.comw.org/pda/0201oef.html.
7. Jonathan Steele, "Forgotten Victims," *The Guardian*, May 20, 2022.
8. Donald H. Rumsfeld, Department of Defense News Briefing, December 4, 2001.
9. Norman Solomon, "Terrorism, 'the War on Terror' and the Message of Carnage," Fairness and Accuracy In Reporting, July 11, 2005, www .fair.org/media-beat-column/terrorism-8220the-war-on-terror8221 -and-the-message-of-carnage.
10. Joan Didion, "Fixed Opinions, or the Hinge of History," *New York Review of Books*, January 16, 2003.
11. David Vine et al., "Creating Refugees: Displacement Caused by the United States' Post-9/11 Wars," Costs of War, Watson Institute, Brown University, September 8, 2020, watson.brown.edu/costsofwar/files/ cow/imce/papers/2020/Displacement_Vine%20et%20al_Costs%20 of%20War%202020%2009%2008.pdf.
12. Neta C. Crawford and Catherine Lutz, "Human Cost of Post-9/11 Wars: Direct War Deaths in Major War Zones, Afghanistan and Pakistan (Oct. 2001–Aug. 2021); Iraq (March 2003–Aug. 2021); Syria

(Sept. 2014–May 2021); Yemen (Oct. 2002–Aug. 2021) and Other Post-9/11 War Zones," Costs of War, Watson Institute, Brown University, September 1, 2021, watson.brown.edu/costsofwar/figures/2021/WarDeathToll.

13. George W. Bush, "Remarks by the President," White House, September 14, 2001.

14. "Not in Our Names," Institute for Public Accuracy, September 27, 2001, www.accuracy.org/release/881-not-in-our-names.

15. George W. Bush, "President Bush Addresses the Nation," White House, September 20, 2001.

16. "Not in Our Names."

17. Amber Amundson, "A Widow's Plea for Non-Violence," *Common Dreams*, September 25, 2001.

18. "Sept. 11, 2001: Orlando and Phyllis Rodriguez: 'Not in Our Son's Name,'" This Day in History, Zinn Education Project, www.zinnedproject.org/news/tdih/orlando-and-phyllis-rodriguez-not-in-our-sons-name.

19. "Not in Our Names."

20. "Opponents of Terrorism and War," Institute for Public Accuracy, October 1, 2001, www.accuracy.org/release/883-opponents-of-terrorism-and-war.

21. David W. Moore, "Public Overwhelmingly Backs Bush in Attacks on Afghanistan," Gallup, October 8, 2001, news.gallup.com/poll/4966/public-overwhelmingly-backs-bush-attacks-afghanistan.aspx.

22. Norman Solomon, "The Media Protest Too Much," *New York Times*, May 24, 1991.

23. From the poem "September 1, 1939"; W.H. Auden, *Another Time* (New York: Random House, 1940).

24. John Newhouse, *Imperial America: The Bush Assault on the World Order* (New York: Vintage, 2003), 47.

25. "100,000 Iraqis Died, Allied Officer Says," Associated Press, March 23, 1991; "Remembering the Gulf War: Key Facts and Figures about the Conflict," *Forces Network*, February 28, 2021, www.forces.net/news/remembering-gulf-war-key-facts-figures; Patrick E. Tyler, "After the War; Powell Says U.S. Will Stay in Iraq 'for Some Months,'" *New York Times*, March 23, 1991.

26. Jon Jackson, "Watch: Madeleine Albright Saying Iraqi Kids' Deaths 'Worth It' Resurfaces," *Newsweek*, March 23, 2022, newsweek.com/watch-madeleine-albright-saying-iraqi-kids-deaths-worth-it-resurfaces-1691193. See also: Jon Schwarz, "RIP Madeleine Albright and Her Awful, Awful Career," *The Intercept*, March 25, 2022.

27. Madeleine K. Albright, "Prepared Statement before the Senate Foreign Relations Committee," January 8, 1997.

28. Tom Gjelten, "Iraq Resolution Timeline," *All Things Considered*, NPR, November 8, 2002.

29. Obama's brief Afghanistan visit in March 2010 was a grim counterpoint to the day in 1966 when another president, in the midst of escalating another war, also took a long ride on Air Force One to laud and inspire the troops. In South Vietnam, at Cam Ranh Bay, President Lyndon Johnson told the American fighters: "Be sure to come home with that coonskin on the wall." Then, too, thousands of soldiers responded to the president's exhortations by whooping it up. And then, too, the media coverage was upbeat. In a cover story written by an eminent journalist of the era, Shana Alexander, *Life* quoted a corporal who called Johnson's visit the "best morale booster Cam Ranh's ever had." The magazine piece went on: "Certainly the corporal was right and so was [White House press secretary Bill] Moyers when he later compared the day to a sermon, in that so much of the real meaning is not in what the preacher says but in what his listeners hear." The article concluded that it had been a "wild and quite wonderful day." (*Life*, November 4, 1966.)

30. Norman Solomon, "Obama in a Bomber Jacket," *Truthout*, March 29, 2010.

31. Alissa J. Rubin and Helene Cooper, "In Afghan Trip, Obama Presses Karzai on Graft," *New York Times*, March 28, 2010.

32. Barack Obama, "Address to the Troops in Afghanistan," White House, March 28, 2010.

33. Stephanie Savell, "The 2001 Authorization for Use of Military Force: A Comprehensive Look at Where and How It Has Been Used," Costs of War, Watson Institute, Brown University, December 14, 2021, www.watson.brown.edu/costsofwar/files/cow/imce/papers/2021/Costs%20of%20War_2001%20AUMF.pdf.

34. Neta C. Crawford, Azmat Khan, Nick Turse, Craig Whitlock, and Charles Sennott, "Lessons and Legacies in an Age of Endless War," Ellsberg Conference Panel, University of Massachusetts Amherst, May 1, 2021.

35. "Remarks by President Biden on the End of the War in Afghanistan," White House, August 31, 2021.

36. "Human Cost of Post-9/11 Wars: Direct War Deaths in Major War Zones," Costs of War, Watson Institute, Brown University, September 1, 2021.

37. Martin Luther King Jr., "The World House (excerpt)," Beacon Broad-

side: A Project of Beacon Press, January 18, 2010, www.beaconbroad
side.com/broadside/2010/01/martin-luther-king-jr-the-world-house-
excerpt.html.

38. "Praise, Protest as U.S. Recalls King Legacy," Associated Press, January 19, 2004.

Chapter One REPETITION AND OMISSION

1. Ashik Siddique, "The U.S. Spends More on Its Military Than the Next
10 Countries Combined," National Priorities Project, April 30, 2020,
www.nationalpriorities.org/blog/2020/04/30/us-spends-military-
spending-next-10-countries-combined.

2. Jason Lemon, "As Congress Debates Military Budget, U.S. to Spend
More Than Next 10 Countries Combined," *Newsweek*, July 22, 2020.

3. "U.S. Military Bases Overseas: The Facts," Overseas Base Realign-
ment and Closure Coalition, www.overseasbases.net/fact-sheet.html.

4. David Vine, Patterson Deppen, and Leah Bolger, "Drawdown: Improving U.S. and Global Security through Military Base Closures Abroad,"
Quincy Institute for Responsible Statecraft, September 20, 2021,
quincyinst.org/report/drawdown-improving-u-s-and-global-security-
through-military-base-closures-abroad.

5. Vine, Deppen, and Bolger, "Drawdown."

6. Katrina vanden Heuvel and Robert L. Borosage, "The Head of Every
Table: Joe Biden's Impossible Foreign Policy Aspirations," *The Nation*,
February 16, 2021.

7. Edward Jay Epstein, *Between Fact and Fiction* (New York: Vintage,
1975), 218.

8. Fred Friendly quoted in Michael X. Delli Carpini, "Vietnam and the
Press," in *The Legacy: The Vietnam War and the American Imagination*, ed. D. Michael Shafer (Boston: Beacon Press, 1990), 139.

9. Daniel Hallin, *The "Uncensored War": The Media and Vietnam*
(Berkeley: University of California Press, 1989), 107.

10. Michael Herr, *Dispatches* (New York: Vintage International, 1977), 215.

11. "Collateral Murder," WikiLeaks, April 5, 2010, collateralmurder
.wikileaks.org.

12. Mark Crispin Miller, *Boxed In: The Culture of TV* (Evanston, IL:
Northwestern University Press, 1988), 157.

13. Susan Sontag, *Regarding the Pain of Others* (New York: Farrar, Straus
and Giroux, 2003), 13, 38.

14. Norman Solomon, "The Media Protest Too Much," *New York Times*,
May 24, 1991.

15. Dan Rather, CBS, February 27, 1991, quoted in Greg Dawson and Sentinel Television Critic, "A Different War for Press Corps," *Orlando Sentinel*, March 3, 1991.

16. Sontag, *Regarding the Pain*, 66.

17. Tim Arango, "After 25 Years of U.S. Role in Iraq, Scars Are Too Stubborn to Fade," *New York Times*, February 16, 2016.

18. Martin A. Lee and Norman Solomon, *Unreliable Sources: A Guide to Detecting Bias in News Media* (New York: Carol, 1992), paperback edition, xix.

19. Jim Naureckas, "Gulf War Coverage," Fairness and Accuracy In Reporting, April 1, 1991, www.fair.org/extra/gulf-war-coverage.

20. Loretta Alper and Jeremy Earp, directors, *War Made Easy* (Media Education Foundation, 2007), documentary film.

21. Alper and Earp, *War Made Easy.*

22. David Vaina, "The Vanishing Embedded Reporter in Iraq," Pew Research Center, October 26, 2006.

23. Alper and Earp, *War Made Easy.*

24. Alper and Earp, *War Made Easy.*

25. Darcy G. Richardson, *A Nation Divided: The 1968 Presidential Campaign* (Bloomington, IN: iUniverse, 2002), 8.

26. Norman Solomon, "Where Is the Voice of Dissent?," *Los Angeles Times*, August 2, 2002.

27. Victor Navasky and Christopher Cerf, "Who Said the War Would Pay for Itself? They Did!," *The Nation*, March 13, 2008.

28. Powell speaking in interview with French network TV2; transcript released by U.S. Department of State, September 12, 2003.

29. Matt Corley, "Abizaid: 'We've Treated the Arab World as a Collection of Big Gas Stations,'" *ThinkProgress*, October 15, 2007, archive.think progress.org/abizaid-weve-treated-the-arab-world-as-a-collection-of-big-gas-stations-cb2612fcd0bd.

30. Bonnie Bricker, Erik Leaver, and Adil E. Shamoo, "The Costs of War for Oil," Foreign Policy in Focus, October 19, 2007, fpif.org/the_costs_of_war_for_oil.

31. Bricker, Leaver, and Shamoo, "Costs of War for Oil."

32. Andrew E. Kramer, "In Rebuilding Iraq's Oil Industry, U.S. Subcontractors Hold Sway," *New York Times*, June 16, 2011.

33. Antonia Juhasz, "Why the War in Iraq Was Fought for Big Oil," CNN.com, April 15, 2013.

34. "Al-Qaeda Terrorist Attacks by Number of Deaths from 1993 to 2010," Statista, May 2011, www.statista.com/statistics/272757/al-qaeda-terrorist-attacks-by-death-toll; U.S. Department of State, "Country Reports on Terrorism," 2009–2017.

35. Nick Turse, "A Blank Check for Endless War," *TomDispatch*, January 4, 2022, tomdispatch.com/the-war-on-terror-is-a-success-for-terror.

36. George H.W. Bush, "Remarks to the American Legislative Exchange Council," March 1, 1991, www.presidency.ucsb.edu/documents /remarks-the-american-legislative-exchange-council-0.

37. On April 20, 1999, the nation was shocked by a massacre at Columbine High School in Colorado. A pair of seniors used shotguns and other weaponry to kill twelve fellow students and a teacher. At the time, it was the highest death toll from a mass shooting at a high school in the United States. Underscoring the cruel derangement was the fact that the assailants even made some bombs to plant at the school. The tragedy at Columbine occurred on the twenty-eighth straight day of the U.S.-led NATO bombing of Yugoslavia that killed five hundred civilians, many of them children, according to Human Rights Watch (www.hrw.org/news/2000/02/07/new-figures-civilian-deaths-kosovo-war); the Yugoslav government said the number of civilians killed was much higher. Missiles hit schools, hospitals, factories, bridges, and stores. At the outset of the bombing, President Bill Clinton declared in a televised address, "Our thoughts and prayers tonight must be with the men and women of our armed forces, who are undertaking this mission for the sake of our values and our children's future." A few weeks later, on television again, Clinton was deploring what happened at Columbine, on a day when the bombing of Yugoslavia happened to be heavier than ever. "We do know," the president said, "that we must do more to reach out to our children and teach them to express their anger and to resolve their conflicts with words, not weapons." The utterly conflicting assertions from the president merited scrutiny in tandem. But in the irony-free zone of war-desensitized media, such contradictions would be far too uncomfortable to explore.

Chapter Two OVER THE HORIZON

1. Valerie Hopkins, Steven Erlanger, and Michael Schwirtz, "Russian Rocket Barrage Kills Civilians as First Talks Show No Progress," *New York Times*, February 28, 2022.

2. "Horror Grows Over Slaughter in Ukraine," *New York Times*, April 5, 2022.

3. David Tapia, "Invasion News Fits on Front Page More When an Enemy Does the Invading," Fairness and Accuracy In Reporting, June 9, 2022, fair.org/home/invasion-news-fits-on-front-page-more-when-an-enemy-does-the-invading.

4. Harlan Ullman and James Wade Jr., *Shock & Awe: Achieving Rapid Dominance* (Washington, DC: Institute for National Strategic Studies, 1996), 37.

5. Colin Powell, *My American Journey* (New York: Random House, 1995), 207.

6. John T. Correll, "What Happened to Shock and Awe?," *Air Force Magazine*, November 1, 2003, www.airforcemag.com/article/1103shock.

7. Harlan Ullman and Arnaud de Borchgrave, "Shock and Awe in Ukraine? Not Yet," United Press International, March 2, 2022.

8. The U.S.-led coalition had succeeded in forcing Iraqi troops out of Kuwait, ending Iraq's six-month occupation that interrupted the monarchical rule by an extremely wealthy family in control of the small emirate. As journalist Len Ackland wrote at the time in an unusual opinion piece for the *Chicago Tribune*, "there is no democracy to restore in Kuwait," since it was "a feudal, oil-rich oligarchy operated for the benefit of the ostentatious al-Sabah royal family." And: "Iraq violated international law by invading Kuwait and overthrowing its leadership. The United States violated international law by invading Panama and overthrowing its leadership. While two wrong invasions do not make either right, the similarity of these displays of brute force should make [President George H.W.] Bush reconsider the self-righteous statements he has been making." The piece was published on August 29, 1990.

9. Patrick E. Tyler, "After the War; Powell Says U.S. Will Stay in Iraq 'for Some Months,'" *New York Times*, March 23, 1991.

10. Tyler, "After the War." While making Powell a national hero, the Gulf War also gave a big boost to the popularity of the commander in chief, George H.W. Bush. The president's poll numbers had sagged in the latter months of 1990—but beginning with the war's launch by U.S.-led forces in mid-January 1991, the upward climb of Bush's popularity was so fast and steep that it created a nearly vertical long line on Gallup's "presidential job approval" graph. The polling organization later reported: "Bush's approval rating surged from 64 percent the week prior to the start of military action to 82 percent right after it, staying high throughout the war. After victory in the war, in March of that year, Bush received an 89 percent approval rating, the highest presidential job approval rating ever recorded to that date." (R.J. Reinhardt, "George H.W. Bush Retrospective," Gallup, December 1, 2018, news.gallup.com/opinion/gallup/234971/george-bush-retrospective.aspx.) Public enthusiasm was stoked by the fact that the military triumph mainly relied on an air war, and so many more Iraqis died than

Americans; 154 was the official number of U.S. combat deaths. (J.C. Helmkamp, "United States Military Casualty Comparison during the Persian Gulf War," *Journal of Occupational and Environmental Medicine* 36, no. 6, June 1994: 609–15.) With rare exceptions, sizable U.S. media outlets were not any more interested in the Iraqi deaths than General Powell was.

11. Dexter Filkins, "Over Baghdad: Wary Targets, Yet Confident," *New York Times*, November 17, 2003.

12. Ever since the War Powers Act became law in 1973, Congress has rarely invoked it and no president has ever agreed to be constrained by it. Federal courts have refused to order presidential adherence.

13. Bruce Ackerman, "Legal Acrobatics, Illegal War," *New York Times*, June 20, 2011.

14. Paul Starobin, "A Moral Flip-Flop? Defining a War," *New York Times*, August 6, 2011.

15. "Testimony by Legal Adviser Harold Hongju Koh, U.S. Department of State, on Libya and War Powers, before the Senate Foreign Relations Committee," June 28, 2011, 2009–2017.state.gov/documents/organ ization/167452.pdf. See also: David A. Fahrenthold, "Obama Adviser Makes Case to Senate Panel for Involvement in Libya," *Washington Post*, June 28, 2011.

16. Starobin, "Moral Flip-Flop?"

17. Starobin, "Moral Flip-Flop?"

18. David Vine, Patterson Deppen, and Leah Bolger, "Drawdown: Improv- ing U.S. and Global Security through Military Base Closures Abroad," Quincy Institute for Responsible Statecraft, September 20, 2021, quincyinst.org/report/drawdown-improving-u-s-and-global-security- through-military-base-closures-abroad.

19. "Combined Forces Air Component Commander 2011–2016 Airpower Statistics," U.S. Air Forces Central Command, March 31, 2016.

20. Nick Turse, "AFRICOM Becomes a 'War-Fighting Combatant Com- mand,'" *TomDispatch*, April 13, 2014, tomdispatch.com /nick-turse-africom-becomes-a-war-fighting-combatant-command.

21. "Air Force Gains 18 New Pilots During SUPT Class 16-05 Graduation at Vance," Vance Air Force Base, February 19, 2016.

22. Rick Moriarty, "Reaper Drones Make History, Fly Unescorted In and Out of Syracuse Airport," Syracuse.com, September 27, 2019, syracuse .com/news/2019/09/reaper-drones-make-history-fly-unescorted-in- and-out-of-syracuse-airport.html.

23. Mark Weiner, "Syracuse Has Nation's Highest Poverty Concentrated among Blacks, Hispanics," Syracuse.com, September 6, 2015, syracuse

.com/news/2015/09/syracuse_has_nations_highest_poverty_concen-trated_among_blacks_hispanics.html.

24. Stephen Miles (@SPMiles42), "The U.S. has sought to bring 'peace and stability' to Iraq with airstrikes or bombings in: 1991, 1992, 1993, 1996, 1998, 1999, 2000, 2001, 2002, 2003, 2004, 2005, 2006, 2007, 2008, 2009, 2010, 2011, 2014, 2015, 2016, 2017, 2018, 2019, 2020, 2021: It's time we recognize we cannot bomb our way to peace," Twitter, June 28, 2021, 11:11 a.m., twitter.com/spmiles42/status/1409529908800413698.

25. As the classic military theorist Carl von Clausewitz observed, "a conqueror is always a lover of peace." Clausewitz, *On War*, bk. 6, chap. 5, "Character of the Strategic Defensive" (1873), www.clausewitz.com/readings/OnWar1873/BK6ch05.html#:~:text=A%20conqueror%20is%20always%20a,which%20must%20defend%20itself%2C%20which.

26. "Remarks by President Biden on the End of the War in Afghanistan," White House, August 31, 2021.

27. Ben Armbruster, "Report: Weapons Industry Pocketed at Least $4.4 Trillion Since 9/11," Quincy Institute for Responsible State-craft, September 13, 2021, responsiblestatecraft.org/2021/09/13/report-weapons-industry-pocketed-at-least-4-4-trillion-since-9-11.

28. William D. Hartung and Leila Riazi, "Executive Excess: CEO Compensation in the Arms Industry," Center for International Policy, May 2021, 3ba8a190-62da-4c98-86d2-893079d87083.usrfiles.com/ugd/3ba8a1_53cf880837cd4b178a80adfd0f00812f.pdf.

29. "Reed, Inhofe Praise Senate Passage of National Defense Authorization Act for Fiscal Year 2022," press release, Senate Committee on Armed Services, December 15, 2021.

30. "Reed, Inhofe Praise Senate Passage."

31. Connor O'Brien, "Senators Tack $45B onto Biden's Defense Budget," *Politico*, June 16, 2022.

32. Jane Arraf, Sangar Khaleel, and Eric Schmitt, "U.S. Troops Join Assault on Prison Where ISIS Holds Hostage Hundreds of Boys," *New York Times*, January 25, 2022.

33. Fionnuala Ní Aoláin, "Position of the United Nations Special Rapporteur on the Promotion and Protection of Human Rights and Fundamental Freedoms while Countering Terrorism on the Human Rights of Adolescents/Juveniles Being Detained in North-East Syria," Special Procedures of the Human Rights Council, May 2021, www.ohchr.org/sites/default/files/Documents/Issues/Terrorism/SR/UNSRCT_Position_human-rights-of-boys-adolescents-2021_final.pdf.

34.　Tess Bridgeman and Brianna Rosen, "Still at War: The United States in Syria," Just Security, April 29, 2022, www.justsecurity.org/81313/still-at-war-the-united-states-in-syria.

35.　"U.S. Troops Join Assault on Prison Where ISIS Holds Hostage Hundreds of Boys," *New York Times*, January 25, 2022.

36.　Tess Bridgeman and Brianna Rosen, "Introduction to Symposium: Still at War—Where and Why the United States Is Fighting the 'War on Terror,'" Just Security, March 24, 2022, www.justsecurity.org/80800/introduction-to-symposium-still-at-war-where-and-why-the-united-states-is-fighting-the-war-on-terror.

37.　Bridgeman and Rosen, "Still at War." See also: Rukmini Callimachi, "ISIS Affiliate Claims October Attack on U.S. Troops in Niger," *New York Times*, January 13, 2018.

38.　Kathryn Watson, Sara Cook, Ed O'Keefe, and David Martin, "Biden Details U.S. Raid That Took Out 'Horrible Terrorist' ISIS leader in Syria," CBS News, February 4, 2022; Peter Grantiz and Brian Naylor, "Biden Says ISIS Leader Is Dead After U.S. Operation," NPR, February 3, 2022.

39.　Chantal Da Silva, Ammar Cheikh Omar, Courtney Kube, and Phil Helsel, "ISIS Leader Dies During U.S. Special Forces Raid in Syria, Biden Says," NBC News, February 3, 2022.

40.　Jon Finer, interview by Judy Woodruff, "Biden's Deputy National Security Adviser on U.S. Raid in Syria, Tensions with Russia," *PBS NewsHour*, February 3, 2022.

41.　Robert Burns, "Austin Orders More Focus on Limiting Civilian Casualties," Associated Press, January 27, 2022. See also: Eric Schmitt, Charlie Savage, and Azmat Khan, "Austin Orders Overhaul to Better Protect Civilians During U.S. Combat Operations," *New York Times*, August 25, 2022.

42.　Hina Shamsi, "ACLU Statement on Pentagon's New Civilian Harm Directive," January 27, 2022, www.aclu.org/press-releases/aclu-statement-pentagons-new-civilian-harm-directive.

43.　Peter Maass, "Pentagon Professes Shock That U.S. Airstrikes Frequently Kill Civilians," *The Intercept*, January 29, 2022.

44.　Jake Johnson, "6 Children Reportedly Killed During U.S. Raid in Syria," *Common Dreams*, February 3, 2022.

Chapter Three UNINTENDED DEATHS

1.　Mark Thompson, "Iraq: Urban Warfare: How to Squeeze a City," *Time*, April 19, 2004.

2. Neta C. Crawford and Catherine Lutz, "Human Cost of Post-9/11 Wars: Direct War Deaths in Major War Zones, Afghanistan and Pakistan (Oct. 2001–Aug. 2021); Iraq (March 2003–Aug. 2021); Syria (Sept. 2014–May 2021); Yemen (Oct. 2002–Aug. 2021) and Other Post–9/11 War Zones," Costs of War, Watson Institute, Brown University, September 1, 2021, watson.brown.edu/costsofwar/figures/2021/WarDeathToll.

3. Thomas L. Friedman, "America's Multiple-Choice Quiz," *New York Times*, January 31, 1998.

4. Thomas L. Friedman, "Rattling the Rattler," *New York Times*, January 19, 1999.

5. Thomas L. Friedman, "More Sticks," *New York Times*, April 6, 1999.

6. Thomas L. Friedman, "Stop the Music," *New York Times*, April 23, 1999.

7. Steven Lee Myers and Elizabeth Becker, "As Leaders Meet, NATO Air Campaign Enters 2d Month," *New York Times*, April 25, 1999.

8. Friedman, "Stop the Music."

9. Chronicle News Services, "NATO Attack Misfires—15 Civilians Die," *San Francisco Chronicle*, May 8, 1999.

10. John Simpson, "Hearts and Minds Are Not Won Like This," *Sunday Telegraph*, May 9, 1999.

11. Paul Watson, "Unexploded Weapons Pose Deadly Threat on Ground," *Los Angeles Times*, April 28, 1999.

12. In his 957-page memoir, published five years after NATO's lengthy bombing blitz, Bill Clinton's account of the war made no mention of cluster weaponry and devoted one sentence to civilian deaths. "The bombs would inflict great damage on the military and economic infrastructure of Serbia," he wrote. "Alas, on a few occasions they would miss their intended targets and take the lives of people we were trying to protect." The former president used the inadvertently ironic phrase "under fire" while praising his vice president, secretary of state, and national security adviser when he recalled the gratifying victory won by the seventy-eight days of intensive bombing: "Al Gore, Madeleine Albright, and Sandy Berger had all remained cool under fire in the nail-biting, roller-coaster weeks we had just been through together." Bill Clinton, *My Life* (New York: Knopf, 2004), 851, 859.

13. "Cluster Munitions: Background and Issues for Congress," Congressional Research Service, March 9, 2022, sgp.fas.org/crs/weapons/RS22907.pdf.

14. Valerie Hopkins, Steven Erlanger, and Michael Schwirtz, "Rocket Assaults Kill Civilians in Ukraine as Tightening Sanctions Isolate Moscow," *New York Times*, March 1, 2022.

15. Lara Jakes and Steven Erlanger, "NATO Accuses Russia of Using Cluster Bombs in Ukraine," *New York Times*, March 4, 2022. The next week, on March 9, the *Times* published a news article headlined "Cluster Munitions and 'Vacuum Bombs': Russian Invasion Revives an Old Debate," which mentioned in passing in its tenth paragraph: "The Convention on Cluster Munitions, which took effect in 2010, bans their use because of the harm they pose to noncombatants. More than 100 nations have signed the treaty, but the United States, Ukraine and Russia have not."

16. Olivia Riggio, "NBC Off by 18 Years on U.S.'s Last Use of Cluster Bombs," Fairness and Accuracy In Reporting, March 3, 2022, fair .org/home/action-alert-nbc-off-by-18-years-on-uss-last-use-of-cluster-bombs. For viewer numbers, see Mark Joyella, "Ukraine Coverage Drives Ratings Gains for Cable News, but Broadcast Networks Draw Largest Audience," *Forbes*, March 8, 2022.

17. When the *New York Times Magazine* devoted a lengthy spread to the U.S. military's use of cluster weaponry, the focus was not on civilians but on friendly fire (John Ismay, "America's Dark History of Killing Its Own Troops with Cluster Munitions," December 4, 2019).

18. "Yemen: Images of Missile and Cluster Munitions Point to U.S. Role in Fatal Attack," Amnesty International, June 7, 2010, www.amnesty. org/en/latest/press-release/2010/06/yemen-images-missile-and-cluster-munitions-point-us-role-fatal-attack-2010.

19. Washington tried to hide its responsibility for the 2009 cluster-bomb attack in Yemen. Implausible deniability was the game: on June 7, 2010, CNN described "a new classified agreement with the Yemeni government that the two countries will work together and that the United States will remain publicly silent on its role in providing intelligence and weapons to conduct strikes" (www.cnn.com/2010/WORLD/meast/06/07/yemen.missiles/index.html).

20. *Bill Moyers Journal*, PBS, January 30, 2009.

21. "Pierre Sprey and Marilyn Young on Strategic Bombing," *Bill Moyers Journal*, January 30, 2009.

22. Saeed Shah and Peter Beaumont, "U.S. Drone Strikes in Pakistan Claiming Many Civilian Victims, Says Campaigner," *The Guardian*, July 17, 2011.

23. David Rohde, "The Drone Wars," Reuters, January 26, 2012.

24. Jesselyn Radack, Brandon Bryant, and Michael Haas, "Air Force Whistleblowers Risk Prosecution to Warn Drone War Kills Civilians, Fuels Terror," *Democracy Now!*, November 20, 2015.

25. Sonia Kennebeck, director, *National Bird* (Ten Forward Films, 2016), documentary film.

26. Emran Feroz, "After 20 Years of Drone Strikes, It's Time to Admit They've Failed," *MIT Technology Review*, October 7, 2021.

27. Andrew Cockburn, "Tunnel Vision," *Harper's Magazine*, February 2014.

28. Stand with Daniel Hale, standwithdanielhale.org.

29. Jeremy Scahill et al., "The Drone Papers," *The Intercept*, 2015.

30. Nicola Abé, "The Woes of an American Drone Operator," *Der Spiegel*, December 14, 2012.

31. Heather Linebaugh, "I Worked on the U.S. Drone Program. The Public Should Know What Really Goes On," *The Guardian*, December 29, 2013.

32. Andrew Cockburn, *Kill Chain: The Rise of the High-Tech Assassins* (New York: Henry Holt, 2015), 200.

33. After a successful Freedom of Information Act request, the *New York Times* (January 19, 2022) released twenty-five minutes of video taken from a pair of drones before, during, and after the air attack that took the lives of seven children and three other civilians in Kabul on August 29, 2021. "Disclosure of the videos was a rare step by the U.S. military in any case of an airstrike that caused civilian casualties," the *Times* reported. The newspaper described what had occurred as "a botched U.S. drone strike" that was "a tragic blunder." The reporting concluded that the video showed "the military made a life-or-death decision based on imagery that was fuzzy, hard to interpret in real time and prone to confirmation bias."

34. Gibran Naiyyar Peshimam, "Afghan Family Decimated by U.S. Drone Strike Awaits Justice from Washington," Reuters, November 10, 2021.

35. Tom Vanden Brook, "Air Force Inspector General Says U.S. Strike That Killed 7 Children, 3 Adults in Afghanistan Was 'an Honest Mistake,'" *USA Today*, November 3, 2021.

36. Karoun Demirjian and Alex Horton, "Pentagon Won't Punish Any Troops Over Errant Drone Strike in Kabul That Killed 10 Civilians," *Washington Post*, December 13, 2021.

37. Dave Brown (@Dave_brown24), "Kirby on the drone strike in Kabul that killed civilians: 'We acknowledged that there were procedural breakdowns, processes were not executed the way they should have been. But it doesn't necessarily indicate that an individual or individuals have to be held to account for that,'" Twitter, December 15, 2021, 9:31 a.m., twitter.com/dave_brown24/status/1471125871717146632.

38. "Sentencing Statement by Daniel Hale," Stand with Daniel Hale, standwithdanielhale.org/sentencing-statement.html.

Chapter Four MEDIA BOUNDARIES

1. Jim Rutenberg, "From Cable Star to Face in the Crowd," *New York Times*, May 5, 2003.
2. Itay Hod, "Inside Ashleigh Banfield's Rise and Fall and Rise—Now without Her Signature Glasses," *The Wrap*, October 17, 2016, www .thewrap.com/ashleigh-banfield-rise-fall-hln-glasses.
3. Jim Rutenberg, "At MSNBC, a Young Anchor for Younger Viewers," *New York Times*, October 29, 2001.
4. Rutenberg, "At MSNBC, a Young Anchor."
5. Rutenberg, "Cable Star to Face in the Crowd."
6. Norman Solomon, "The Occasional Media Ritual of Lamenting the Habitual," *Free Press*, October 15, 2005, freepress.org/article/ occasional-media-ritual-lamenting-habitual; Timothy Dumas, "Truth and Consequences: Meet Ashleigh Banfield," *New Canaan Darien*, January–February 2009, web.archive.org/web/20150217100254/http ://www.newcanaandarienmag.com/n/January-2009/Truth-and-Consequences/index.php?cparticle=4&siarticle=3#artanc.
7. Hod, "Ashleigh Banfield's Rise and Fall and Rise."
8. Andrew Grossman, "NBC's Banfield Chided Over Criticisms," *Hollywood Reporter*, April 29, 2003, poynter.org/reporting-editing/2003/ nbcs-banfield-chided-over-criticisms.
9. Dumas, "Truth and Consequences."
10. *Bill Moyers Journal*, PBS, April 3, 2009.
11. George Orwell, *The Collected Essays, Journalism and Letters of George Orwell: As I Please, 1943–1945* (New York: Harcourt, 1968), 181.
12. Norman Solomon and Reese Erlich, *Target Iraq: What the News Media Didn't Tell You* (New York: Context Books, 2003), 12–14.
13. Joshua Rothman, "The Iraq War in The New Yorker," *New Yorker*, March 20, 2013.
14. David Remnick, "Making a Case," *New Yorker*, January 27, 2003.
15. Elana Schor, "Saddam Hussein Had No Direct Ties to al-Qaida, Says Pentagon Study," *The Guardian*, March 12, 2008.
16. Daniel Lazare, "The New Yorker Goes to War," *The Nation*, May 15, 2003.
17. Claire Cozens, "*New York Times*: We Were Wrong on Iraq," *The Guardian*, May 26, 2004. See also: Ruurt Wiegant, "Apologies or Evasions: A Critical Look at the *New York Times*'s and the *Washington Post*'s Self-Criticism," aspeers 9 (2016), www.aspeers.com/node/151?-fulltext. Wiegant's study concluded: "The most prominent self-criticism in the apologies, that of burying critical articles deep in the paper

and critical comments and counterarguments deep in stories, may be true, but is disingenuous for underplaying the relative lack of these elements in general, as shown in the quantitative analysis. Furthermore, some of the reasons the *Washington Post* cites as causing their deficient reporting are not plausible since they also should have affected the publishing of prowar articles as much as antiwar articles. A more convincing set of reasons, then, is the strongly prowar editorial attitude, which the *Washington Post*'s apology puzzlingly both acknowledges and denies, and an uncritical attitude of following conventional wisdom. The *New York Times* rightly criticizes itself for not having questioned the motivations of their Iraqi sources more thoroughly, but neglects to acknowledge that they also uncritically published the opinions of U.S. government officials. Neither paper mentions the negative framing of opponents of the war, the one-sided questioning of their motives, the portrayal of the war as inevitable, or the lack of coverage of both the consequences of the proposed war for the Iraqi people and the legality of the war, which were all shown to be recurring themes in my analysis. Lastly, both papers are undeservedly self-congratulatory about their general reporting. Hence, the apologies of the *New York Times* and the *Washington Post* underplay the deficiency of their coverage, at least for the investigated period from February 6 to 10, 2003, which was more biased and biased in more ways with regards to the run-up to war than their apologies acknowledge."

18. Thomas L. Friedman, "The Chant Not Heard," *New York Times*, November 30, 2003.

19. Thomas L. Friedman, interview by Charlie Rose, *Charlie Rose*, PBS, May 30, 2003.

20. Norman Solomon, "Thomas Friedman Claims It's 'Stupid and Obnoxious' to Say He Was a Cheerleader for the Iraq War," *HuffPost*, August 20, 2013.

21. "Domestic Box Office for 2014," boxofficemojo.com/year/2014/?grossesOption=totalGrosses.

22. Manohla Dargis and A.O. Scott, "The 10 Most Influential Films of the Decade (and 20 Other Favorites)," *New York Times*, November 18, 2020.

23. Stephen Galloway, "Clint Eastwood Describes His Near-Death Experience, Says 'American Sniper' Is Anti-War," *Hollywood Reporter*, March 16, 2015.

24. Charles Thorp, "Jason Hall: Why I Wrote 'American Sniper,'" *Rolling Stone*, January 28, 2015.

25. The plots of *The Green Berets* and *American Sniper* both allowed a dissenting voice— a shaggy-haired journalist, skeptical of the war in

Vietnam, and Kyle's wife, skeptical of the war in Iraq—before each saw the light as part of the third act.

26. Viet Thanh Nguyen, "Vietnamese Lives, American Imperialist Views, Even in 'Da 5 Bloods,'" *New York Times*, June 24, 2020.

27. James Baldwin, *The Fire Next Time* (New York: Dial Press, 1963).

28. Azmat Khan, "Hidden Pentagon Records Reveal Patterns of Failure in Deadly Airstrikes," *New York Times*, December 18, 2021.

29. Michael Levenson, "What to Know about the Civilian Casualty Files," *New York Times*, December 20, 2021.

30. "Shoddy Mainstream Media Coverage of Afghanistan Has Created a Safe Haven for Bad Foreign Policy Ideas," Security Policy Reform Institute, August 27, 2021, www.securityreform.org/commentary/afghanistan-shoddy-media-coverage-bad-foreign-policy.

31. Jim Lobe, "Three Major Networks Devoted a Full Five Minutes to Afghanistan in 2020," Quincy Institute for Responsible Statecraft, August 20, 2021, responsiblestatecraft.org/2021/08/20/three-major-networks-devoted-a-full-five-minutes-to-afghanistan-in-2020.

32. Julie Hollar, "Missing Voices in Broadcast Coverage of Afghan Withdrawal," Fairness and Accuracy In Reporting, September 24, 2021, fair.org/home/missing-voices-in-broadcast-coverage-of-afghan-withdrawal.

33. Richard Engel, MSNBC, *The 11th Hour with Brian Williams*, August 16, 2021.

34. Norah O'Donnell, *CBS Evening News*, August 16, 2021.

35. Jim Lobe, "Out of Sight, Out of Mind: Afghanistan Vanishes from U.S. News," Quincy Institute for Responsible Statecraft, December 29, 2021, responsiblestatecraft.org/2021/12/29/out-of-sight-out-of-mind-afghanistan-vanishes-from-us-news.

36. Lobe, "Out of Sight."

37. Lobe, "Out of Sight."

38. Julie Hollar, "Media Forget Afghan Plight as U.S. Sanctions Drive Mass Famine Risk," Fairness and Accuracy In Reporting, December 21, 2021, fair.org/home/media-forget-afghan-plight-as-us-sanctions-drive-mass-famine-risk.

39. "Time Running Out to Address Afghanistan's Hunger Crisis," Human Rights Watch, March 17, 2022.

40. Robin Wright, "Amid Skepticism, Biden Vows a New Era of Global Collaboration," *New Yorker*, September 21, 2021.

41. Brown University, "Costs of the 20-Year War on Terror: $8 Trillion and 900,000 Deaths," September 1, 2021, brown.edu/news/2021-09-01/costsofwar.

42. Mike Stone, "Biden Wants $813 Billion for Defense as Ukraine Crisis Raises Alarm," Reuters, March 28, 2022.

43. Julie McCarthy, "4 Things to Know after the Philippines Kept Its Pact with the U.S. Military," NPR, August 6, 2021.

44. For instance, listening to CNN's decades-long Pentagon correspondent Barbara Starr has been akin to hearing a Defense Department spokesperson pretend to be a journalist. See Jeremy Scahill, "CNN Blames the Photos, Not the Torture," Antiwar.com, February 16, 2006, original.antiwar.com/scahill/2006/02/16/cnn-blames-the-photos-not-the-torture.

Chapter Five "HUMANE" WARS

1. Julie Hollar, "Missing Voices in Broadcast Coverage of Afghan Withdrawal," Fairness and Accuracy In Reporting, September 24, 2021, fair.org/home/missing-voices-in-broadcast-coverage-of-afghan-withdrawal.

2. "'Humane': Yale Historian Samuel Moyn on 'How the United States Abandoned Peace and Reinvented War,'" *Democracy Now!*, September 9, 2021.

3. Anand Gopal, "The Other Afghan Women," *New Yorker*, September 6, 2021.

4. Anand Gopal, "The Other Afghan Women: Rural Areas Hope Taliban Rule Will End Decades of U.S. and Warlord Violence," *Democracy Now!*, September 16, 2021. See also: "Afghanistan War: UN Says More Civilians Killed by Allies Than Insurgents," BBC News, July 30, 2019.

5. Gopal, "Other Afghan Women: Rural Areas."

6. Chris Hedges, *What Every Person Should Know about War* (New York: Free Press, 2003), 7.

7. Samuel Moyn, "America Is Giving the World a Disturbing New Kind of War," *New York Times*, September 3, 2021.

8. Samuel Moyn, *Humane: How the United States Abandoned Peace and Reinvented War* (New York: Farrar, Straus and Giroux, 2021), 4–5. A major theme of the book is that efforts to halt the worst atrocities of the U.S. post-9/11 wars have been a diversion from the need to stop the wars entirely—in effect presenting a false choice, as though those two goals were in conflict and could not be wisely pursued at the same time.

9. Moyn, *Humane*, 8.

10. Lyndon B. Johnson, "Remarks to Members of the Armed Forces at Cam

Ranh Bay, Vietnam," October 26, 1966, presidency.ucsb.edu/documents/remarks-members-the-armed-forces-cam-ranh-bay-vietnam.

11. Victor Brooks, "Lyndon Johnson in Vietnam: The Turning Point of the '60s," *Salon*, December 2, 2017.

12. Earlier in 1966, Johnson had met in Honolulu with the commander of U.S. forces in Vietnam, William Westmoreland. Using a favorite expression that he would later publicly utilize as an injunction to rank-and-file troops, the president told the general to "nail the coonskin to the wall." What exactly did that mean? No one could say with certainty. A coonskin would belong to an animal: a raccoon, to be precise. (See Larry Berman and Jason Newman, "The Vietnam War and Its Impact," Encyclopedia.com, www.encyclopedia.com/social-sciences/encyclopedias-almanacs-transcripts-and-maps/vietnam-war-and-its-impact.)

13. Johnson, "Remarks to Members of the Armed Forces."

14. "President Obama Delivers Remarks to Soldiers during Surprise Afghanistan Trip," CNN, March 28, 2010, transcript, cnn.com/TRANSCRIPTS/1003/28/bn.01.html.

15. "President Obama Delivers Remarks."

16. "President Obama Delivers Remarks."

17. "Remarks by President Obama in Address to the Nation from Afghanistan," White House, May 1, 2012.

18. "Remarks by President Obama."

19. Ron Kovic, "The Forgotten Wounded of Iraq," *Truthdig*, January 18, 2006, www.truthdig.com/dig/the-forgotten-wounded-of-iraq.

20. James Dao, "No Food for Thought: The Way of the Warrior," *New York Times*, May 16, 2009.

21. Michael Hastings, "The Runaway General: The Profile That Brought Down McChrystal," *Rolling Stone*, June 22, 2010.

22. Tessa Stuart, "Obama Publishes Account of Firing Gen. McChrystal on the Same Day McChrystal Briefs Biden," *Rolling Stone*, November 17, 2020.

23. Charles Bailey et al., "Ramp Up U.S. Engagement with War Legacies in Southeast Asia," Henry L. Stimson Center, May 12, 2021, stimson.org/2021/ramp-up-u-s-engagement-with-war-legacies-in-southeast-asia.

24. George Black, "The Victims of Agent Orange the U.S. Has Never Acknowledged," *New York Times*, March 22, 2021. See also: Fred A. Wilcox, *Scorched Earth: Legacies of Chemical Warfare in Vietnam* (New York: Seven Stories Press, 2011).

25. "The Vietnam War," United States Foreign Policy: History and

Resource Guide, Peace History Society, peacehistory-usfp.org/
vietnam-war.

26. Charles Ornstein, "Agent Orange Act Was Supposed to Help Vietnam
Veterans—but Many Still Don't Qualify," *ProPublica*, July 17, 2015.
See also: Fred A. Wilcox, *Waiting for an Army to Die: The Tragedy
of Agent Orange* (New York: Vintage, 1983). A second edition ·
appeared nearly three decades later (New York: Seven Stories Press,
2011).

27. Norman Solomon and Reese Erlich, *Target Iraq: What the News
Media Didn't Tell You* (New York: Context Books, 2003), 58–59.

28. Samuel Oakford, "Iraq War Records Reignite Debate Over U.S. Use of
Depleted Uranium," *New Humanitarian*, October 6, 2016, thenew
humanitarian.org/investigations/2016/10/06/exclusive-iraq-war-
records-reignite-debate-over-us-use-depleted-uranium.

29. Elena Bruess, Joe Snell, Anne Snabes, and Madhurita Goswami, "War
and the Environment: The Disturbing and Under-Researched Legacy
of Depleted Uranium Weapons," *Bulletin of the Atomic Scientists*,
2020, thebulletin.org/2020/07/war-and-the-environment.

30. Jessica Shiu, Joanna Gaitens, Katherine S. Squibb, Patricia W. Gucer,
Melissa A. McDiarmid, and Anthony A. Gaspari, "Significance of Der-
matologic Findings in a Cohort of Depleted Uranium–Exposed Veterans
of Iraqi Conflicts," *Dermatitis* 26, no. 3 (May–June, 2015): 142–47.

31. Jennifer Lubell, "IOM Report Links Illness, Gulf War Service,"
Modern Healthcare, April 9, 2010, modernhealthcare.com/
article/20100409/NEWS/304099962/iom-report-links-illness-
gulf-war-service.

32. "Remarks of President Joe Biden—State of the Union Address as Prepared for Delivery," White House, March 1, 2022.

33. Joseph Hickman, "Burn Pits: U.S. Government Ignores 60,000 Suffering U.S. War Vets," *Truthout*, May 29, 2016.

34. Jessica Dean, Clare Foran, and Shawna Mizelle, "House Passes
Amended Burn Pit Legislation," CNN, July 13, 2022.

35. Seung Min Kim and Matt Viser, "Biden Calls for Legislation to Help
Sick Veterans Who Served Near Burn Pits," *Washington Post*, March
8, 2022.

36. Jessica Dean and Ali Zaslav, "Senate Passes Long-Sought Bill to Help
Veterans Affected by Burn Pits," CNN, August 2, 2022.

37. Pat Elder, email to author, March 10, 2022.

38. "Fact Sheet: Continued U.S. Support for a Peaceful, Stable
Afghanistan," White House, June 25, 2021; "20 Years of U.S. Military
Aid to Afghanistan," Stockholm International Peace Research

Institute, September 22, 2021, www.sipri.org/commentary/topical-backgrounder/2021/20-years-us-military-aid-afghanistan; "How Much Did the U.S. Spend in Aid to Afghanistan?," USA Facts, September 3, 2021, usafacts.org/articles/how-much-did-the-us-spend-in-aid-to-afghanistan.

39. Brian Osgood, "A Million Afghan Children Could Starve This Winter. Are U.S. Sanctions to Blame?," *The Nation*, December 23, 2021.

40. "Afghanistan on 'Countdown to Catastrophe' without Urgent Humanitarian Relief," UN News, United Nations, October 25, 2021.

41. Christina Goldbaum, "Facing Economic Collapse, Afghanistan Is Gripped by Starvation," *New York Times*, December 4, 2021.

42. Jane Ferguson, "Afghanistan Has Become the World's Largest Humanitarian Crisis," *New Yorker*, January 5, 2022.

43. Saphora Smith, "U.S. Announces Fresh $308 Million in Humanitarian Aid for Struggling Afghans," NBC News, January 11, 2022.

44. Kelly Cobiella, Ahmed Mengli, Petra Cahill, and Yuka Tachibana, "'The Situation Is Dire': Inside Afghanistan's 'Fast Unraveling' Humanitarian Crisis," NBC News, January 31, 2022.

45. "Letter to President Biden Regarding Afghanistan's Humanitarian and Economic Crisis," December 20, 2021, progressives.house.gov/_cache/files/7/9/79c380ca-661d-4158-9a88-f3a67ca24cdd/C36F3C117B0CAB34701D29E87BE22083.12-20-21-afghanistan-humanitarian-crisis-letter-2-.pdf.

46. Charlie Savage, "Spurning Demand by the Taliban, Biden Moves to Split $7 Billion in Frozen Afghan Funds," *New York Times*, February 11, 2022.

47. Joe Biden, "Executive Order on Protecting Certain Property of Da Afghanistan Bank for the Benefit of the People of Afghanistan," February 11, 2022, www.whitehouse.gov/briefing-room/presidential-actions/2022/02/11/executive-order-on-protecting-certain-property-of-da-afghanistan-bank-for-the-benefit-of-the-people-of-afghanistan.

48. Mehdi Hasan (@Mehdirhasan), "I cannot describe for you in words how outrageous this is. Afghans are starving, this is all *their* money, and there was not a single Afghan aboard any of those 4 planes on 9/11. 15 Saudis, plus Egyptian, Emirati, Lebanese nationals. Get the money from those countries if you must," Twitter, February 11, 2022, 8:15 a.m., twitter.com/mehdirhasan/status/1492125240129953803?lang=en.

49. Austin Ahlman, "Biden's Decision on Frozen Afghanistan Money Is Tantamount to Mass Murder," *The Intercept*, February 11, 2022.

50. Ahlman, "Biden's Decision."

51. Bernie Sanders (@SenSanders), "Afghanistan is facing a humanitarian catastrophe. I urge the Biden administration to immediately release billions in frozen Afghan government funds to help avert this crisis, and prevent the death of millions of people," Twitter, January 18, 2022, 3:22 p.m., twitter.com/sensanders/status/1483535342095458316?lang=en.

52. Ahlman, "Biden's Decision."

53. Ahlman, "Biden's Decision."

54. Julie Hollar, "Biden's Multi-Billion Afghan Theft Gets Scant Mention on TV News," Fairness and Accuracy In Reporting, February 15, 2022, fair.org/home/bidens-multi-billion-afghan-theft-gets-scant-mention-on-tv-news.

55. Hollar, "Biden's Multi-Billion Afghan Theft."

56. "Afghanistan: Nearly 20 Million Going Hungry," UN News, United Nations, May 9, 2022.

57. Bryce Greene, "NPR Devotes Almost Two Hours to Afghanistan Over Two Weeks—and Thirty Seconds to U.S. Starving Afghans," Fairness and Accuracy In Reporting, September 2, 2022, fair.org/home/npr-devotes-almost-two-hours-to-afghanistan-over-two-weeks-and-30-seconds-to-us-starving-afghans. See also: Julie Hollar, "Biden's Afghan Shell Game Prompts Media Shrugs and Stenography," Fairness and Accuracy In Reporting, September 20, 2022, fair.org/home/bidens-afghan-shell-game-prompts-media-shrugs-and-stenography.

Chapter Six LIVES THAT REALLY MATTER, LIVES THAT DON'T

1. Howard Kurtz, "CNN Chief Orders 'Balance' in War News," Washington Post, October 31, 2001.

2. Kurtz, "CNN Chief Orders 'Balance.'"

3. Matt Wells, "CNN to Carry Reminders of U.S. Attacks," The Guardian, November 1, 2001.

4. Loretta Alper and Jeremy Earp, directors, War Made Easy (Media Education Foundation, 2007), documentary film.

5. William Dean Howells's short story "Editha" first appeared in Harper's Monthly (January 1905).

6. Barack Obama, "Address to the Troops in Afghanistan," White House, March 28, 2010.

7. Dana Milbank, "Curtains Ordered for Media Coverage of Returning Coffins," Washington Post, October 21, 2003.

8. "Obama Administration Lifts Blanket Ban on Media Coverage of the Return of Fallen Soldiers," National Security Archive, February 26, 2009.

9.   "Obama Administration Lifts Blanket Ban."

10. Matthew Duss and Peter Juul, "The Iraq War Ledger (2013 Update)," Center for American Progress, March 19, 2013, www.american progress.org/article/the-iraq-war-ledger-2013-update.

11. Duss and Juul, "Iraq War Ledger."

12. George Bush (@GeorgeHWBush), "Very much regret missing the Memorial Day parade today in Kennebunkport, and am forever grateful not only to those patriots who made the ultimate sacrifice for our Nation—but also the Gold Star families whose heritage is imbued with their honor and heroism," Twitter, May 28, 2018, 5:02 p.m., twitter.com/GeorgeHWBush/status/1001222316653776897?cxt= HHwWgsC81Y2Zh-UbAAAA.

13. "Remembering the Gulf War: Key Facts and Figures about the Conflict," Gulf War, *Forces Network*, February 28, 2021.

14. "President Bush Marks Veterans Day at National Fallen Soldiers Memorial Ceremony," White House, November 11, 2007.

15. "Collateral Murder," WikiLeaks, April 5, 2010, collateralmurder. wikileaks.org. Two Reuters journalists were among the eleven civilians killed, while two children were gravely wounded. "Leaked U.S. Video Shows Deaths of Reuters' Iraqi Staffers," Reuters, April 5, 2010. See also: Paul Daley, "'All Lies': How the U.S. Military Covered Up Gunning Down Two Journalists in Iraq," *The Guardian*, June 14, 2020.

16. Jessica Corbett, "UN Expert Calls Detention of Chelsea Manning 'Open-Ended, Progressively Severe, Coercive Measure Amounting to Torture,'" *Common Dreams*, December 31, 2019.

17. "Chelsea Manning and Her Attorneys File Motion Declaring She Will Never Cooperate with Grand Jury," Sparrow Project, May 6, 2019, sparrowmedia.net/2019/05/chelsea-manning-and-her-attorneys-file-motion-declaring-she-will-never-cooperate-with-grand-jury.

18. Anthony J. Trenga, "In the United States District Court for the Eastern District of Virginia: Order," March 12, 2020.

19. Thalif Deen, "World's Worst Humanitarian Disaster Triggered by Deadly Weapons from U.S. and U.K.," Inter Press Service, March 8, 2021, www.globalissues.org/news/2021/03/08/27369.

20. "Yemen Crisis: What You Need to Know," UNICEF, Summer 2022, www.unicef.org/emergencies/yemen-crisis.

21. "End the War on Yemen," Just Foreign Policy, www.justforeignpolicy .org/end-the-war-on-yemen.

22. Anna Foster, "Saudi Arabia: The Significance of Biden's Fist Bump with Crown Prince," BBC News, July 16, 2022.

23. Julian E. Barnes, "CIA Concludes That Saudi Crown Prince Ordered

Khashoggi Killed," *New York Times*, November 16, 2018; Julian E. Barnes and David E. Sanger, "Saudi Crown Prince Is Held Responsible for Khashoggi Killing in U.S. Report," *New York Times*, February 26, 2021.

24. Ben Norton, "MSNBC Ignores Catastrophic U.S.-Backed War in Yemen," Fairness and Accuracy In Reporting, January 8, 2018, fair .org/home/msnbc-yemen-russia-coverage-2017.

25. Amanda Hess, "This Is the Moment Rachel Maddow Has Been Waiting For," *New York Times Magazine*, December 7, 2020.

26. "At Doom's Doorstep: It Is 100 Seconds to Midnight," *Bulletin of the Atomic Scientists*, January 20, 2022, thebulletin.org/doomsday-clock.

27. Lawrence Korb and Stephen Cimbala, "Why the War in Ukraine Poses a Greater Nuclear Risk Than the Cuban Missile Crisis," Just Security, April 12, 2022, www.justsecurity.org/81040/why-the-war-in-ukraine-poses-a-greater-nuclear-risk-than-the-cuban-missile-crisis.

28. "At Doom's Doorstep."

29. Albert Einstein, Letter to "Emergency Committee of Atomic Scientists Incorporated," January 22, 1947, sgp.fas.org/eprint/einstein.html.

30. "The Anti-Ballistic Missile (ABM) Treaty at a Glance," Arms Control Association, December 2020, www.armscontrol.org/factsheets/ abmtreaty.

31. "Anti-Ballistic Missile (ABM) Treaty."

32. Shannon Bugos, "U.S. Completes INF Treaty Withdrawal," Arms Control Association, September 2019, www.armscontrol.org/ act/2019-09/news/us-completes-inf-treaty-withdrawal.

33. Andrew Cockburn, *The Spoils of War: Power, Profit and the American War Machine* (London: Verso Books, 2021), 78. Kennan was far from the only establishment eminence on foreign policy to vehemently oppose NATO expansion. On June 26, 1997, with enlargement of NATO on the near horizon, a prophetic open letter to then president Bill Clinton warned that "the current U.S.-led effort to expand NATO" was "a policy error of historic proportions." The letter added: "We believe that NATO expansion will decrease allied security and unsettle European stability." The signers were fifty prominent figures in foreign policy circles—including a half dozen former senators, former Defense secretary Robert McNamara, and such mainstream luminaries as Susan Eisenhower, Townsend Hoopes, Fred Ikle, Edward Luttwak, Paul Nitze, Richard Pipes, Stansfield Turner, and Paul Warnke. www.armscontrol.org/act/1997-06/arms-control-today/ opposition-nato-expansion.

34. Alison Mutler, "NATO Shows Off Missile Base in Romania, Calling It 'Purely Defensive,'" Radio Free Europe/Radio Liberty, November 25,

2019, www.rferl.org/a/nato-shows-off-missile-base-in-romania-calling-it-purely-defensive-/30291193.html.

35. William J. Perry, "Why It's Safe to Scrap America's ICBMs," *New York Times*, September 30, 2016.

36. Daniel Ellsberg and Norman Solomon, "To Avoid Armageddon, Don't Modernize Missiles—Eliminate Them," *The Nation*, October 19, 2021.

37. David Jackson and Savannah Behrmann, "Dick Cheney, Once a Villain to Democrats, Hailed in Surprise Capitol Visit to Mark Jan. 6," *USA Today*, January 6, 2022.

38. Marianna Sotomayor and Paul Kane, "Dick Cheney Returns to the House and Receives a Warm Welcome . . . from Democrats," *Washington Post*, January 6, 2022.

39. Lisa Respers France, "Ellen DeGeneres Explains Hanging Out with Her Friend George W. Bush," CNN, October 8, 2019.

40. Samantha Schnurr, "Ellen DeGeneres Responds to Criticism Over Sitting with George W. Bush," *E! News*, October 8, 2019.

41. Todd Garrin, "Michelle Obama Says She and George W. Bush 'Disagree on Policy' but Their 'Values Are the Same,'" Yahoo Entertainment, December 10, 2019.

Chapter Seven THE COLOR OF WAR

1. "Media Coverage of Ukraine: When Selectivity Becomes Propaganda," Institute for Public Accuracy, March 3, 2022, accuracy.org/release/media-coverage-of-ukraine-when-selectivitybecomes-propaganda.

2. Fairness and Accuracy In Reporting, *Extra!* newsletter, April 2022.

3. Eoin Higgins, "'Relatively Civilized, Relatively European': Media Bias Infects Coverage of Ukraine War," *The Flashpoint*, February 28, 2022, eoinhiggins.substack.com/p/relatively-civilized-relatively-european?utm_source=url&s=r.

4. Higgins, "'Relatively Civilized.'"

5. "Statement in Response to Coverage of the Ukraine Crisis," Arab and Middle Eastern Journalists Association, February 2022.

6. Lorraine Ali, "In Ukraine Reporting, Western Press Reveals Grim Bias Toward 'People Like Us,'" *Los Angeles Times*, March 2, 2022.

7. Nick Turse, "The Forgotten People of a Fictional Country," *TomDispatch*, March 3, 2022, tomdispatch.com/war-torn.

8. Turse, "Forgotten People."

9. Peter Beinart, "We Can Support Ukraine and Admit the Racism in U.S. Foreign Policy at the Same Time," *Beinart Notebook*, March 7, 2022, peterbeinart.substack.com/p/we-can-support-ukraine-and-admit.

10. James J. Zogby, "About Double Standards," Arab American Institute, March 7, 2022, www.aaiusa.org/library/about-double-standards.

11. Matt Duss (@MattDuss), "As a Ukrainian-American I am immensely proud of the bravery of Ukrainians and of the support being shown by Americans. As a Middle East analyst I am floored by the blatant double standard on resisting occupation and repression," Twitter, February 28, 2022, 8:27 a.m., twitter.com/mattduss/status/1498288661976264707.

12. Gideon Levy, "The Israeli Kettle and the Russian Pot," *Haaretz*, February 27, 2022.

13. "'High Time for Accountability,' UN Expert Says as Israel Approves Highest Rate of Illegal Settlements," UN News, October 30, 2020, news.un.org/en/story/2020/10/1076572.

14. Amnesty International, "Crime of Apartheid: The Government of Israel's System of Oppression Against Palestinians," www.amnesty usa.org/endapartheid; Human Rights Watch, "A Threshold Crossed: Israeli Authorities and the Crimes of Apartheid and Persecution," April 27, 2021, www.hrw.org/report/2021/04/27/threshold-crossed/israeli-authorities-and-crimes-apartheid-and-persecution; B'Tselem, "A Regime of Jewish Supremacy from the Jordan River to the Mediterranean: This Is Apartheid," January 12, 2021, www.btselem.org/publications/fulltext/202101_this_is_apartheid.

15. Peter Baker and Julie Hirschfeld Davis, "U.S. Finalizes Deal to Give Israel $38 Billion in Military Aid," *New York Times*, September 13, 2016.

16. Zogby, "About Double Standards."

17. Kelebogile Zvobgo and Meredith Loken, "Why Race Matters in International Relations," *Foreign Policy*, June 19, 2020.

18. Gurminder K. Bhambra et al., "Why Is Mainstream International Relations Blind to Racism?," *Foreign Policy*, July 3, 2020.

19. Nima Gerami, "To Defeat Systemic Racism, America Must End Endless War," Quincy Institute for Responsible Statecraft, July 5, 2020, responsiblestatecraft.org/2020/07/05/to-defeat-systemic-racism-america-must-end-endless-war.

20. Nick Turse, "Another U.S.-Trained Soldier Stages a Coup in West Africa," *The Intercept*, January 26, 2022.

21. Turse, "Another U.S.-Trained Soldier."

22. Karoun Demirjian and Danielle Paquette, "Biden Sending Hundreds of U.S. Troops to Somalia, Reversing Trump," *Washington Post*, May 16, 2022. The article vaguely noted in passing that the U.S. had been bombing the country: "Army Gen. Stephen Townsend, head of U.S. Africa Command, warned lawmakers earlier this year that the

U.S. withdrawal from Somalia had hampered the military's ability to suppress the threat there, saying that undertaking so-called 'over the horizon' strikes launched from a permanent base in neighboring Djibouti was akin to 'commuting to work.'"

23. Nick Turse, "Will the Biden Administration Shine Light on Shadowy Special Ops Programs?," *The Intercept*, March 20, 2021.

24. Turse, "Will the Biden Administration Shine Light."

25. Nick Turse, "America's Commandos: What Did They Do and Where Did They Do It?," *TomDispatch*, March 19, 2020, tomdispatch.com/nick-turse-america-s-commandos-what-did-they-do-and-where-did-they-do-it.

26. "Who We Are," Movement for Black Lives, m4bl.org/about-us/who-we-are.

27. Robbie Shilliam, "When Did Racism Become Solely a Domestic Issue?," *Foreign Policy*, June 23, 2020.

28. "Rate of Fatal Police Shootings in the United States from 2015 to June 2022, by Ethnicity," Statista, 2015–2022, statista.com/statistics/1123070/police-shootings-rate-ethnicity-us.

29. "The Color of Justice: Racial and Ethnic Disparity in State Prisons," Sentencing Project, 2021, www.sentencingproject.org/wp-content/uploads/2016/06/The-Color-of-Justice-Racial-and-Ethnic-Disparity-in-State-Prisons.pdf.

30. John Templon, "Police Departments Have Received Hundreds of Millions of Dollars in Military Equipment Since Ferguson," BuzzFeed, June 4, 2020.

31. Sven Gustafson, "Pentagon Armed Police with Billions in Vehicles, Weapons," *Autoblog*, June 8, 2020, autoblog.com/2020/06/08/surplus-military-vehicles-weapons-police-departments; Dan Parsons, "Repurposed MRAPs Find New Life in Police Agencies," *National Defense Magazine*, April 2014, web.archive.org/web/20141202045901/http:/www.nationaldefensemagazine.org/archive/2014/April/Pages/RepurposedMRAPsFindNewLifeinPoliceAgencies.aspx.

32. Brian Barrett, "The Pentagon's Hand-Me-Downs Helped Militarize Police. Here's How," *Wired*, June 2, 2020.

33. Barrett, "Pentagon's Hand-Me-Downs."

34. Hank Johnson, Letter to President Joe Biden on Pentagon's 1033 Program, April 6, 2021. See also: Rebecca Kheel, "House Democrats Push Biden to Limit Transfer of Military-Grade Gear to Police," *The Hill*, April 6, 2021.

35. Joe Biden, "Executive Order on Advancing Effective, Accountable Policing and Criminal Justice Practices to Enhance Public Trust and Public Safety," May 25, 2022.

36. "Rep. Johnson on Two Years After the Senseless Police Murder of George Floyd and President Biden's Executive Order," May 26, 2022, hankjohnson.house.gov/media-center/press-releases/rep-johnson-two-years-after-senseless-police-murder-george-floyd-and.

37. Jessica Katzenstein, "The Wars Are Here: How the United States' Post-9/11 Wars Helped Militarize U.S. Police," Costs of War, Watson Institute, Brown University, September 16, 2020, watson.brown.edu/costsofwar/files/cow/imce/papers/2020/Police%20Militarization_Costs%20of%20War_Sept%2016%202020.pdf.

38. Brenda Gayle Plummer, "Martin Luther King Jr.'s Forgotten Foreign-Policy Vision," *Foreign Policy*, January 18, 2022.

39. Martin Luther King Jr., "Speech on Receipt of Honorary Doctorate in Civil Law," University of Newcastle upon Tyne, November 13, 1967; "Martin Luther King Receives Honorary Degree from Newcastle University," *The Guardian*, November 14, 1967.

40. Martin Luther King Jr., "Beyond Vietnam: A Time to Break Silence," Riverside Church, New York City, April 4, 1967.

41. King, "Beyond Vietnam."

42. King's speech in the early spring of 1967 was ten months before the *Boston Globe* did a survey of thirty-nine major U.S. newspapers and found that not a single one had urged American withdrawal from Vietnam (*Boston Globe*, February 18, 1968).

43. Obery M. Hendricks Jr., "The 'Macroethics' of Martin Luther King Jr.," *Salon*, January 18, 2016.

44. Michael Eric Dyson, *I May Not Get There with You: The True Martin Luther King, Jr.* (New York: Free Press, 2000), 62. The *Newsweek* columnist was Kenneth Crawford.

45. Jeff Cohen, "40 Years Later, (The Late) Martin Luther King Still Silenced," *HuffPost*, April 4, 2008.

46. Viet Thanh Nguyen, "Vietnamese Lives, American Imperialist Views, Even in 'Da 5 Bloods,'" *New York Times*, June 24, 2020.

47. King, "Beyond Vietnam."

48. King, "Beyond Vietnam."

Chapter Eight COSTS OF WAR

1. Lindsay Koshgarian, "What's in the FY 2022 Budget Deal for the Military?," National Priorities Project, March 9, 2022, www.nationalpriorities.org/blog/2022/03/09/whats-fy-2022-budget-deal-military.

2. "We now have more income and wealth inequality than at any time in the last hundred years," Senator Bernie Sanders wrote. "In the year

2022, three multibillionaires own more wealth than the bottom half of American society—160 million Americans. Today, 45 percent of all new income goes to the top 1 percent, and CEOs of large corporations make a record-breaking 350 times what their workers earn. . . . Today we have more concentration of ownership than at any time in the modern history of this country. In sector after sector a handful of giant corporations control what is produced and how much we pay for it." Bernie Sanders, "The U.S. Has a Ruling Class—and Americans Must Stand Up to It," *The Guardian*, September 2, 2022.

3. "Rep. Adam Smith," Top Industries 2019–2020, OpenSecrets.org, www.opensecrets.org/members-of-congress/adam-smith/industries ?cid=N00007833&cycle=2020&type=C.

4. William Stafford, *Every War Has Two Losers: William Stafford on Peace and War*, ed. Kim Stafford (Minneapolis, MN: Milkweed Editions, 2003).

5. David Vine, Patterson Deppen, and Leah Bolger, "Drawdown: Improving U.S. and Global Security through Military Base Closures Abroad," Quincy Institute for Responsible Statecraft, September 20, 2021, quincyinst.org/report/drawdown-improving-u-s-and-global-security-through-military-base-closures-abroad.

6. "Martin Luther King Jr. Day Teach-In," Political Science, Illinois Wesleyan University, 2010–2022, www.iwu.edu/political-science/king-day. html.

7. Lindsay Koshgarian, "U.S. Military Contracts Totaled $3.4 Trillion Over Ten Years," National Priorities Project, October 28, 2021, www.nationalpriorities.org/blog/2021/10/28/us-military-contracts-totaled-34-trillion-over-ten-years.

8. William D. Hartung, "Profits of War: Corporate Beneficiaries of the Post-9/11 Pentagon Spending Surge," Costs of War, Watson Institute, Brown University, September 13, 2021, watson.brown.edu/costsofwar/papers/2021/ProfitsOfWar.

9. "Summary of Findings," Costs of War, Watson Institute, Brown University, watson.brown.edu/costsofwar/papers/summary.

10. Neta C. Crawford and Catherine Lutz, "Human Cost of Post-9/11 Wars: Direct War Deaths in Major War Zones, Afghanistan and Pakistan (Oct. 2001–Aug. 2021); Iraq (March 2003–Aug. 2021); Syria (Sept. 2014–May 2021); Yemen (Oct. 2002–Aug. 2021) and Other Post-9/11 War Zones," Costs of War, Watson Institute, Brown University, September 1, 2021, watson.brown.edu/costsofwar/figures/2021/WarDeathToll.

11. Crawford and Lutz, "Human Cost of Post-9/11 Wars."

12. Crawford and Lutz, "Human Cost of Post-9/11 Wars."

13. "U.S. and Allied Killed," Costs of War, Watson Institute, Brown University, July 2021, watson.brown.edu/costsofwar/costs/human/military/killed.

14. Crawford and Lutz, "Human Cost of Post-9/11 Wars."

15. "Millions Displaced by U.S. Post-9/11 Wars," Costs of War, Watson Institute, Brown University, August 19, 2021, watson.brown.edu/costs ofwar/files/cow/imce/papers/2021/Costs%20of%20War_Vine%20 et%20al_Displacement%20Update%20August%202021.pdf.

16. Stephanie Savell, "United States Counterterrorism Operations 2018–2020," Costs of War, Watson Institute, Brown University, February 2021, watson.brown.edu/costsofwar/papers/2021/USCounterterrorismOperations.

17. Alex Horton and Aaron Gregg, "Use of Military Contractors Shrouds True Costs of War. Washington Wants It That Way, Study Says," *Washington Post*, June 30, 2020.

18. Heidi Peltier, "The Growth of the 'Camo Economy' and the Commercialization of the Post-9/11 Wars," Costs of War, Watson Institute, Brown University, June 30, 2020, watson.brown.edu/costsofwar/papers/2020/growth-camo-economy-and-commercialization-post-911-wars-0.

19. "Top 100 Contractors in Iraq, Afghanistan," Center for Public Integrity, November 19, 2007, publicintegrity.org/national-security/top-100-contractors-in-iraq-afghanistan.

20. Ann Wright, email to author, March 11, 2022.

21. Ellen Ioanes, "More U.S. Contractors Have Died in Afghanistan Than U.S. Troops—but the Pentagon Doesn't Keep Track," *Business Insider*, December 10, 2019, businessinsider.com/more-us-contractors-have-died-in-afghanistan-than-us-troops-2019-12.

22. Wright email.

23. Elizabeth Beaumont, "Rights of Military Personnel," Free Speech Center at Middle Tennessee State University, 2009, mtsu.edu/first-amendment/article/1131/rights-of-military-personnel.

24. Beaumont, "Rights of Military Personnel." It is not only matters involving the free-speech rights of soldiers that the federal judiciary has ruled itself "ill-equipped" to intervene on, thus allowing the military command to lay down its own laws curtailing such rights. On the rare occasions when Congress has voted to directly constrain presidential war making by invoking the War Powers Act, which was passed into law in 1973, the upper reaches of the court system have refused to impede the warfare, leaving the man behind the desk in the Oval Office with a free hand to keep wars going.

25. "Traumatic Brain Injury," Mayo Clinic, mayoclinic.org/diseases-conditions/traumatic-brain-injury/symptoms-causes/syc-20378557.

26. "TBI Among Service Members and Veterans," Centers for Disease Control and Prevention, www.cdc.gov/traumaticbraininjury/military/index.html.

27. Trisha A. Hostetter, Claire A. Hoffmire, Jeri E. Forster, Rachel Sayko Adams, Kelly A. Stearns-Yoder, and Lisa A. Brenner, "Suicide and Traumatic Brain Injury among Individuals Seeking Veterans Health Administration Services between Fiscal Years 2006 and 2015," *Journal of Head Trauma Rehabilitation* 34, no. 5 (2019): E1–E9. In addition, veterans overall have been at higher risk of suicide than the general population. Citing a 2018 report from the Veterans Administration, the study in the *Journal of Head Trauma Rehabilitation* noted that "the suicide rate among veterans was approximately 1.5 times greater than that among civilian adults, after accounting for age and gender." (See also U.S. Department of Veterans Affairs, Office of Mental Health and Suicide Prevention, "VA National Suicide Data Report 2005–2016," issued in 2018.)

28. Jeffrey T. Howard, Ian J. Stewart, Megan Amuan, Jud C. Janak, and Mary Jo Pugh, "Association of Traumatic Brain Injury with Mortality among Military Veterans Serving after September 11, 2001," *JAMA Network Open* 5, no. 2 (February 1, 2022): e2148150.

29. Barbara Ehrenreich, *Blood Rites: Origins and History of the Passions of War* (New York: Metropolitan Books, 1997), 230.

30. Melinda Wenner Moyer, "'A Poison in the System': The Epidemic of Military Sexual Assault," *New York Times*, August 3, 2021.

31. "Senators Gillibrand, Grassley, Ernst, Blumenthal, Cruz, Shaheen, Kelly and Military Sexual Assault Advocates Introduce New, Bipartisan Military Justice Improvement and Increasing Prevention Act," news release from the office of Senator Kirsten Gillibrand, April 29, 2021.

32. "Gillibrand Statement on the Gutting of Bipartisan Miliary Justice Reforms by House and Senate Armed Services Leadership," news release from the office of Senator Kirsten Gillibrand, December 7, 2021.

33. Ellie Kaufman, "Bipartisan Senators Criticize Defense Bill, Saying It Does Not Go Far Enough to Reform Military Justice for Sexual Assault Survivors," CNN, December 8, 2021.

34. Leo Shane III, "Military Sexual Harassment Will Be a Crime Under New White House Executive Order," *Military Times*, January 25, 2022.

35. Stacy Bannerman, "The Fatal 'New Normal' for Wives of Veterans," Women's Media Center, March 8, 2017, womensmediacenter.com/news-features/the-fatal-new-normal-for-wives-of-veterans.

36. For statistics on escalated rates of domestic violence from military personnel, see: Stacy Bannerman, *Homefront 911: How Families of Veterans Are Wounded by Our Wars* (New York: Arcade, 2015).

37. Bannerman, "Fatal 'New Normal.'"

38. U.S. Department of Veterans Affairs, "Women Veterans Health Care: Intimate Partner Violence" (2022), www.womenshealth.va.gov/WOM ENSHEALTH/topics/intimate-partner-violence.asp.

39. Patricia Kime, "Pentagon Needs Better Data on Domestic Abuse in the Military Community, Audit Finds," Military.com, May 17, 2021, www.military.com/daily-news/2021/05/17/pentagon-needs-better-data-domestic-abuse-military-community-audit-finds.html.

40. Kime, "Pentagon Needs Better Data."

41. "The Facts About Abuse in Military Families," DomesticShelters. org, December 2, 2016, www.domesticshelters.org/articles/statistics/ the-facts-about-abuse-in-military-families.

42. "In 2018, about 7 percent of U.S. adults were veterans, down from 18 percent in 1980, according to the Census Bureau." (Pew Research Center, "The Changing Face of America's Veteran Population," April 5, 2021.)

43. Hugh Gusterson, "Veterans and Mass Shootings," letter, *New York Times*, July 21, 2016.

44. Hugh Gusterson, "Understanding Mass Killings," *Sapiens*, July 18, 2016, www.sapiens.org/column/conflicted/mass-killers-military-service.

45. Doug Bandow, "Hillary Clinton Never Met a War She Didn't Want Other Americans to Fight," *Forbes*, September 26, 2016.

46. Ellen Moore, *Grateful Nation: Student Veterans and the Rise of the Military-Friendly Campus* (Durham, NC: Duke University Press, 2017), 197.

47. James Carden, "New Study: The Communities Most Affected by War Turned to Trump in 2016," *The Nation*, July 13, 2017.

48. Douglas L. Kriner and Francis X. Shen, "Battlefield Casualties and Ballot Box Defeat: Did the Bush-Obama Wars Cost Clinton the White House?," Social Science Research Network, June 19, 2017, papers.ssrn. com/sol3/papers.cfm?abstract_id=2989040.

49. Richard Fry, Jeffrey S. Passel, and D'Vera Cohn, "A Majority of Young Adults in the U.S. Live with Their Parents for the First Time Since the Great Depression," Pew Research Center, September 4, 2020.

50. Zack Friedman, "Student Loan Debt Statistics in 2021: A Record $1.7 Trillion," *Forbes*, February 20, 2021.

51. Daniel Kurt, "Student Loan Debt: 2021 Statistics and Outlook," Investopedia, April 9, 2022, www.investopedia.com/student-loan-debt-2019-statistics-and-outlook-4772007.

52. David Dayen, "The Great Escape," *American Prospect*, November 29, 2021.

53. Robert Pollin and Heidi Garrett-Peltier, "The U.S. Employment Effects of Military and Domestic Spending Priorities: 2011 Update," Political Economy Research Institute at University of Massachusetts, Amherst, December 2011.

54. "Study Says Domestic, Not Military Spending, Fuels Job Growth," Brown University, May 25, 2017, www.brown.edu/news/2017-05-25/jobscow.

55. Alexandria Ocasio-Cortez (@AOC), "War is a class conflict, too. The rich and powerful who open war escape the consequences of their decisions. It's not their children sent into the jaws of violence. It is often the vulnerable, the poor, and working people—who had little to no say in conflict—who pay the price," Twitter, January 3, 2020, 4:27 p.m., twitter.com/aoc/status/1213210234732371968?lang=en.

56. "Remarks by Secretary of Defense Lloyd J. Austin III at the Reagan National Defense Forum (As Delivered)," U.S. Department of Defense, December 4, 2021.

57. Tom Dreisbach and Meg Anderson, "Nearly 1 in 5 Defendants in Capitol Riot Cases Served in the Military," *All Things Considered*, NPR, January 21, 2021.

58. U.S. Census Bureau, "Those Who Served: America's Veterans from World War II to the War on Terror," report number ACS-43, June 2, 2020.

59. Michael Biesecker, Jake Bleiberg, and James Laporta, "The War Comes Home: Capitol Mob Included Highly Trained Ex-Military and Cops," Associated Press, January 15, 2021.

60. "Leader of Oath Keepers and 10 Other Individuals Indicted in Federal Court for Seditious Conspiracy and Other Offenses Related to U.S. Capitol Breach," Department of Justice, January 13, 2022.

61. Konstantin Toropin, "Oath Keeper Militia Members Including 5 Veterans Indicted on Sedition Charges for Jan. 6 Riot," Military.com, January 13, 2022, www.military.com/daily-news/2022/01/13/oath-keeper-militia-members-including-5-veterans-indicted-sedition-charges-jan-6-riot.html.

62. Konstantin Toropin and Steve Beynon, "Veterans Make Up Most of Proud Boys Members Indicted on Sedition for Jan. 6 Violence," Military.com, June 7, 2022, www.military.com/daily-news/2022/06/07/veterans-make-most-of-proud-boys-members-indicted-sedition-jan-6-violence.html.

63. "Capitol Hill Siege," GW Program on Extremism, July 21, 2022, extremism.gwu.edu/Capitol-Hill-Siege.

64. "Remarks by the President at the National Defense University," White House, May 23, 2013.
65. Jane Mayer, "Obama's Challenge to an Endless War," *New Yorker*, May 23, 2013.
66. Medea Benjamin and Nicolas J.S. Davies, "Hey, Hey, USA! How Many Bombs Did You Drop Today?," *CounterPunch*, January 13, 2022, www.counterpunch.org/2022/01/13/hey-hey-usa-how-many-bombs-did-you-drop-today.
67. Joe Biden (@JoeBiden), "If we give Donald Trump eight years in the White House, he will forever alter the character of our nation," Twitter, June 22, 2020.
68. Ehrenreich, *Blood Rites*, 132.

Chapter Nine NOW IT CAN BE TOLD

1. Press Briefing by Ari Fleischer, White House, December 5, 2002.
2. Press Briefing by Jen Psaki, White House, February 2, 2022.
3. "Some Critical Media Voices Face Censorship," Fairness and Accuracy In Reporting, April 3, 2003, fair.org/press-release/some-critical-media-voices-face-censorship.
4. "Some Critical Media Voices."
5. Dan Friedman, "Why Are Biden's Spokespeople Being All Authoritarian?," *Mother Jones*, February 3, 2022.
6. Friedman, "Why Are Biden's Spokespeople."
7. Steve Inskeep (@NPRinskeep), "This question, by @ayesharascoe, is a basic, fundamental, professional question reporters commonly ask of anyone. To reply 'believe me, or believe ISIS' is not an answer. This country has tried war on the 'You're with us or against us' model, and it didn't work then either," Twitter, February 3, 2022, 3:06 p.m., twitter.com/NPRinskeep/status/1489329579844059140?ref_src=twsrc%5Etfw.
8. Press Gaggle by Press Secretary Jen Psaki, White House, February 3, 2022.
9. For examples of activists, weapons experts, and journalists who challenged the dominant Iraq-has-WMDs narrative for many months before the March 2003 invasion of Iraq, see Institute for Public Accuracy news releases archived at www.accuracy.org; Steve Rendall, "Wrong on Iraq? Not Everyone," Fairness and Accuracy In Reporting, April 1, 2006, fair.org/extra/wrong-on-iraq-not-everyone; "Iraq and the Media: A Critical Timeline," March 19, 2007, fair.org/take-action/media-advisories/iraq-and-the-media.

10. George W. Bush, "Remarks by the President Upon Arrival," White House, September 16, 2001.

11. "At Doom's Doorstep: It Is 100 Seconds to Midnight," *Bulletin of the Atomic Scientists*, January 20, 2022, thebulletin.org/doomsday-clock/current-time.

12. Dahr Jamail, "James Mattis Is a War Criminal: I Experienced His Attack on Fallujah Firsthand," *Truthout*, December 6, 2016.

13. Josh Gerstein, "Obama: 'We Tortured Some Folks,'" *Politico*, August 2, 2014.

14. Andrew Breiner, "How Obama Blew His Chance to Stop U.S. Torture," *Roll Call*, January 26, 2017, rollcall.com/2017/01/26/how-obama-blew-his-chance-to-stop-u-s-torture.

15. Along with running its own torture chambers, the U.S. government used "extraordinary rendition" to turn some prisoners over to allied regimes to do the torturing. "Under the Bush administration, the U.S. government systematically sent people off to a 'who's who' of nations known to use torture—including Egypt, Syria, Uzbekistan, and Yemen," the ACLU said. "Under the Bush administration's program, the CIA rendered at least hundreds of people to torture in other countries, both in facilities run by foreign intelligence agencies or in CIA-run 'black sites.'" See "Extraordinary Rendition," ACLU, www.aclu.org/issues/national-security/torture/extraordinary-rendition. For chilling in-depth accounts of the U.S. torture program during the "war on terror," see James Risen, *Pay Any Price: Greed, Power, and Endless War* (Boston: Houghton Mifflin Harcourt, 2014); Mark Danner, *Spiral: Trapped in the Forever War* (New York: Simon & Schuster, 2016); Spencer Ackerman, *Reign of Terror: How the 9/11 Era Destabilized America and Produced Trump* (New York: Viking, 2021).

16. Dahr Jamail, "What I Saw in Fallujah," *New Statesman*, November 1, 2007, newstatesman.com/long-reads/2007/11/iraq-fallujah-city-military.

17. Jeff Cohen, "So This Is What It Looks Like When the Corporate Media Opposes a War," *Common Dreams*, February 28, 2022.

18. Anne Gearan, "Clinton Slams Trump as a Dangerous Isolationist in American Legion Speech," *Washington Post*, August 31, 2016.

19. "Read Hillary Clinton's Speech Touting 'American Exceptionalism,'" *Time*, August 31, 2016.

20. Barack Obama, "Remarks by the President at the United States Military Academy Commencement Ceremony," White House, May 28, 2014.

21. Writing about the "indispensable nation" motto, political scientist

Micah Zenko observed in 2014: "Like many foreign policy concepts overwhelmingly endorsed by officials and policy makers, this one has little basis in reality. If you consider everything encompassing global affairs—from state-to-state diplomatic relations, to growing cross-border flows of goods, money, people, and data—there are actually very few activities where America's role is truly indispensable, defined by *Webster's* as 'absolutely necessary.' Nevertheless, the notion clearly has political salience, and has even become something of a mandatory mantra for current and prospective commanders-in-chief." (Micah Zenko, "The Myth of the Indispensable Nation," *Foreign Policy*, November 6, 2014, foreignpolicy.com/2014/11/06/the-myth-of-the -indispensable-nation.)

22. Lee Strasberg, *A Dream of Passion: The Development of the Method* (New York: Plume, 1988); quoted in Richard T. Kelly, *Sean Penn: His Life and Times* (London: Faber and Faber, 2004), vii.
23. James Baldwin, *Nothing Personal* (Boston: Beacon Press, 2021), 10.
24. James Baldwin, *The Cross of Redemption: Uncollected Writings* (New York: Vintage, 2011), 42.

ACKNOWLEDGMENTS

MEMORIES OF PEOPLE I MET IN IRAQ AND AFGHANISTAN challenged me to avoid abstraction while writing this book. What I learned from them was beyond measure.

Experts on key aspects of the U.S. warfare state—Nicolas J.S. Davies, William Hartung, and Ann Wright—generously read drafts of chapters and offered valuable comments. So did Cheryl Higgins, whose editing ideas led to more clarity.

Jeff Cohen pored over versions of the manuscript and suggested many nuanced changes, drawing on his great insights into media and politics.

Extraordinary support for this book project came from T.M. Scruggs, who was enthusiastic from the very beginning.

I've learned a huge amount from conversations with Daniel Ellsberg and from his articles, interviews, and books—imbued with vast knowledge and unwavering integrity.

For more than two decades I've had the pleasure of working with Hollie Ainbinder, Layla Cooper, and Sam Husseini at the Institute for Public Accuracy, a nonprofit that provides journalists with solid information and analysis in contrast to dominant media spin.

I'm also blessed to be a colleague of dedicated activists at RootsAction.org and the RootsAction Education Fund, insisting in word and deed that a better world is not only possible but essential.

This book would probably not exist without the steady encouragement and deft work of literary agent Laura Gross. From the time when *War Made Invisible* was merely a title and concept in my mind, she persistently cleared a path from glimmer to completion.

The New Press welcomed and enhanced this book's possibilities. From the outset, senior editor zakia henderson-brown and publisher Ellen Adler saw the potential to break new ground. Assistant editor Ishan Desai-Geller helped me get oriented to the process. The director of editorial programs, Marc Favreau, proved to be a perceptive editor with astute guidance as the manuscript took shape. When the book moved into production, senior managing editor Maury Botton shed light on each step. And copyeditor Eileen Chetti smoothed the way toward the printer.

When the time came to format sources into endnotes, I asked journalist Harrison Malkin to help out, and he came through with on-deadline accuracy. Roxane Assaf-Lynn also provided timely assistance.

Whatever understanding I could bring to *War Made Invisible* was nurtured by countless discussions, email exchanges, interviews, public forums, and writings. People with lasting impacts on me have included James Abourezk, Loretta Alper, David Barsamian, Medea Benjamin, Phyllis Bennis, Karen Bernal, Dennis Bernstein, James Bradley, Fred Branfman, Brandon Bryant, James Carden, Tim Carpenter, Alice Chan, Noam Chomsky, David Clennon, Delmarie Cobb, Steve Cobble, Andrew Cockburn, Jeff Cohen, Harry Coppola, Walt Curtis, Nicolas J.S. Davies, Phil Donahue, Thomas Drake, Jeremy Earp, Barbara

Ehrenreich, Judith Ehrlich, Daniel Ellsberg, Patricia Ellsberg, Tom Engelhardt, Reese Erlich, Benno Friedman, Pia Gallegos, Charles Glass, Anand Gopal, Anthony Guarisco, Daniel Hale, John Hanrahan, Peter Hart, David Hartsough, William Hartung, Edward S. Herman, Adam Hochschild, Julie Hollar, Sam Husseini, Janine Jackson, Dahr Jamail, James Jennings, Kathy Kelly, Robert Koehler, Sonali Kolhatkar, Ron Kovic, Dennis Kucinich, Martin A. Lee, Lisa Ling, Chelsea Manning, Robert McChesney, Alan Minsky, Bill Moyers, Jim Naureckas, Robert Parry, Steve Rendall, Jeremy Scahill, T.M. Scruggs, George Seldes, Lesley Shiner, Donna Smith, Abba Solomon, Erik Sperling, Roger Stahl, Jeffrey Sterling, Fernando Suarez del Solar, David Swanson, Deborah Thomas, Deborah Toler, Fernando Andres Torres, Nina Turner, Nick Turse, Katrina vanden Heuvel, David Vine, Victor Wallis, Jenny Warburg, Cornel West, Cian Westmoreland, Marcy Winograd, Ann Wright, James Zogby, and David Zupan.

I'm also grateful to my sister Helen and brothers Abba and Eugene.

Many years have gone by since my parents, Miriam and Morris Solomon, passed away. Yet I feel the strong presence of inspiring values that they brought to life. As my mother once said to me, "Dead people can be very real."

I never met a more humanistic reporter than Reese Erlich. During a few of his frequent overseas trips, I was lucky to see him at work in Afghanistan, Iraq, and Iran. He died in 2021, leaving a gap that cannot be filled.

Cheryl Higgins has elevated my life in countless ways. Her wisdom, intelligence, and compassion are ongoing counterpoints to the world's grim follies. Her love continues to sustain me.

INDEX

ABOUT THE AUTHOR

NORMAN SOLOMON is co-founder of RootsAction.org and executive director of the Institute for Public Accuracy. His books include *War Made Easy* and *Made Love Got War*. He lives in the San Francisco area.

PUBLISHING IN
THE PUBLIC INTEREST

Thank you for reading this book published by The New Press; we hope you enjoyed it. New Press books and authors play a crucial role in sparking conversations about the key political and social issues of our day.

We hope that you will stay in touch with us. Here are a few ways to keep up to date with our books, events, and the issues we cover:

+ Sign up at www.thenewpress.com/subscribe to receive updates on New Press authors and issues and to be notified about local events

+ www.facebook.com/newpressbooks

+ www.twitter.com/thenewpress

+ www.instagram.com/thenewpress

Please consider buying New Press books not only for yourself, but also for friends and family and to donate to schools, libraries, community centers, prison libraries, and other organizations involved with the issues our authors write about.

The New Press is a 501(c)(3) nonprofit organization; if you wish to support our work with a tax-deductible gift please visit www.thenewpress.com/donate or use the QR code below.